OXFORD WORLD'S CLASSICS

CHRONICLE OF
THE ABBEY OF BURY ST EDMUNDS

JOCELIN OF BRAKELOND was born in the middle of the twelfth century in Bury St Edmunds, Suffolk. His name connects him with the quarter of the town called 'Brakelond'—there is still a street called 'Short Brackland'. In 1173 he became a monk of the great Benedictine abbey that dominated both the town and the surrounding region of West Suffolk. The abbey was an ancient and venerable Saxon foundation and was dedicated to the martyred East Anglian king, St Edmund, who was buried within the church. Although Jocelin's career began promisingly—he became chaplain and close companion of the abbot for a while—he never rose higher than the position of guest master. At one level his book is the story of his disappointments.

In the mid-1190s Jocelin began to write his memoirs of his life in the abbey, and from then on he added new material at frequent intervals. The resulting chronicle takes the story down to 1202, when the book ends abruptly, possibly because of Jocelin's death. It is a remarkably direct and personal account, containing not only closely observed portraits of his contemporaries and unusually vivid recollections of their deeds and conversations, but also some of Jocelin's most intimate thoughts, which give the work a special value.

DIANA GREENWAY is Senior Research Editor at the Institute of Historical Research in the University of London, where she teaches Palaeography. Among her published work are studies of English noble families and of cathedral clergy in the twelfth and thirteenth centuries.

JANE SAYERS is Reader in Administrative History and Diplomatic at University College London, where she teaches Archive students. She has written articles and books on the medieval papacy and medieval monasteries. Her most recent publication is a collection of essays entitled *Law and Records in Medieval England* (1988).

OXFORD WORLD'S CLASSICS

*For almost 100 years Oxford World's Classics have brought
readers closer to the world's great literature. Now with over 700
titles—from the 4,000-year-old myths of Mesopotamia to the
twentieth century's greatest novels—the series makes available
lesser-known as well as celebrated writing.*

*The pocket-sized hardbacks of the early years contained
introductions by Virginia Woolf, T. S. Eliot, Graham Greene,
and other literary figures which enriched the experience of reading.
Today the series is recognized for its fine scholarship and
reliability in texts that span world literature, drama and poetry,
religion, philosophy and politics. Each edition includes perceptive
commentary and essential background information to meet the
changing needs of readers.*

OXFORD WORLD'S CLASSICS

JOCELIN OF BRAKELOND

Chronicle of the Abbey of Bury St Edmunds

Translated with an Introduction and Notes by
DIANA GREENWAY and JANE SAYERS

Oxford   New York
OXFORD UNIVERSITY PRESS

Oxford University Press, Great Clarendon Street, Oxford OX2 6DP

Oxford New York

Athens Auckland Bangkok Bogotá Buenos Aires Calcutta
Cape Town Chennai Dar es Salaam Delhi Florence Hong Kong Istanbul
Karachi Kuala Lumpur Madrid Melbourne Mexico City Mumbai
Nairobi Paris São Paulo Singapore Taipei Tokyo Toronto Warsaw

and associated companies in Berlin Ibadan

Oxford is a registered trade mark of Oxford University Press

© Diana Greenway and Jane Sayers 1989

First published as a World's Classics paperback 1989
Reissued as an Oxford World's Classics paperback 1998

British Library Cataloguing in Publication Data

Data available

Library of Congress Cataloging in Publication Data
Jocelin, de Brakelond, fl. 1173–1215. [Cronica. English]
Chronicle of the Abbey of Bury St. Edmunds/Jocelin de Brakelond;
translated with an introduction and notes by Diana Greenway and Jane Sayers.
p.   cm.—(Oxford world's classics)—Translation of: Cronica.   Bibliography: p.
1. Abbey of Bury St. Edmunds—History. 2. Abbeys—England—Bury
Saint Edmunds—History. 3. Samson, Abbot of Bury St. Edmunds,
1135–1211. 4. Edmund, King of East Anglia, 841–870. 5. Bury Saint
Edmunds (England)—History. 6. Great Britain—History—Angevin
period, 1154–1216. 7. England—Church history—Medieval period, 1066–1485.
I. Greenway, Diana E.   II. Sayers, Jane E.   III. Title.   IV. Series.
BX2595.B78J63   1989   271′.1′042644—dc19   88–18635
ISBN 0–19–283895–4 (pbk.)

1 3 5 7 9 10 8 6 4 2

Printed in Great Britain by
The Bath Press, Bath

CONTENTS

BURY ST EDMUNDS AT THE TIME OF JOCELIN

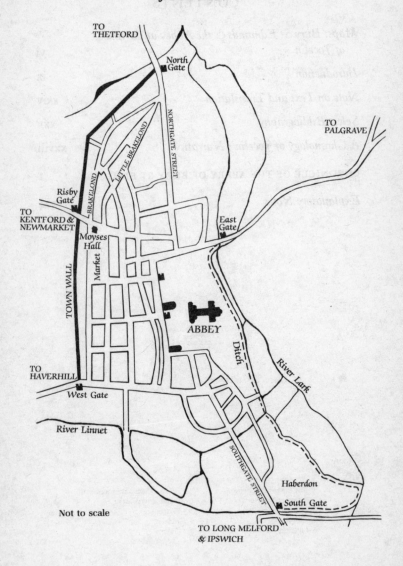

TO THETFORD

North Gate

TO PALGRAVE

LITTLE BRAKELOND

NORTHGATE STREET

BRAKELOND

Risby Gate

TO KENTFORD & NEWMARKET

East Gate

Moyses Hall

Market

TOWN WALL

ABBEY

Ditch

River Lark

TO HAVERHILL

West Gate

River Linnet

SOUTHGATE STREET

Not to scale

Haberdon

South Gate

TO LONG MELFORD & IPSWICH

THE PLAN OF THE ABBEY AT THE TIME OF JOCELIN

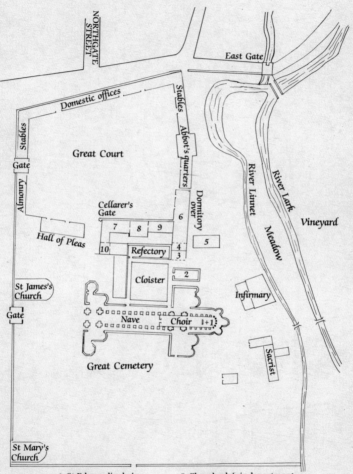

NORTHGATE STREET

East Gate

Domestic offices

Stables

Abbot's quarters

Stables

Gate

Great Court

Almonry

Dormitory over

Cellarer's Gate

6

7 8 9

5

River Linnet

River Lark

Vineyard

Meadow

Hall of Pleas

10 Refectory

4
3

St James's Church

Cloister

2

Infirmary

Gate

Nave Choir 1+1

Sacrist

Great Cemetery

St Mary's Church

1 St Edmund's shrine	6 Chamberlain's department
2 Chapter-house	(under dormitory)
3 Warming-house	7 Cellarer
4 Pittancery	8 Kitchen
5 Lavatories	9 Larder
	10 Guest master

INTRODUCTION

JOCELIN OF BRAKELOND'S *Chronicle* takes us to the heart of the medieval world. His monastery of Bury St Edmunds was not a withdrawn community, secluded and segregated from ordinary life, such as the modern mind conjures up, but a centre of political power and influence. For over 500 years St Edmund's abbey dominated East Anglia, an area rich from its farmland and highly populated. Local and regional government came under the abbey, which was also the landlord of extensive estates. The monks owned and controlled the town, the market, the mills, the hospitals, and the inns. As Jocelin tells us, the community impinged on every activity, charitable, educational, and commercial. The abbey was famed throughout England: it was known also in Europe, from Scandinavia to Italy. Both King Henry II and King John visited St Edmund's, and judges, earls, barons, and archbishops frequently found their way there from London or Norwich, or from the Continent via Ipswich, Felixstowe, and other eastern ports.

The abbot of St Edmund's was a man of power, and not simply within his region, where he acted as the king's vice-gerent. He had frequent contact with the royal court. Medieval government was conducted from the saddle and out of the travelling chest, and all rulers and administrators, even kings, were peripatetic. Samson, as abbot, was a tireless traveller on horseback and on foot. As feudal lord and king's representative, he regularly toured his manors and visited the villages of West Suffolk. He was often in the midlands and south, and frequently travelled to and from London—sometimes meeting important persons on the road, as we know from Jocelin's account of his chance encounter with Archbishop Hubert Walter. He was present at the siege of Windsor, went to Germany to seek out

Richard I, and later attended the king in Normandy. Had the king allowed him, he would have joined the Third Crusade and gone with the Christian forces to the Holy Land. Before he became abbot, he had been on missions in the abbey's service as far afield as Durham in the north and the papal curia in Italy. Having the status of bishop in his own area, the abbot of St Edmund's ranked with the great men of Europe, wielding power, influencing the external world. In a distinguished succession of abbots, some of them born and brought up in France and in Italy, men of culture and standing, who were the confidants of kings, Samson brought the outside world to Bury.

It is our particular good fortune that Bury produced a writer of the calibre of Jocelin at a time when it had a vigorous and colourful abbot, a man who on any judgement wielded his great powers with greatness. It is doubtless the force of Samson's personality that is responsible for Jocelin's *Chronicle*. Although the work has its moral purpose— as we gather on the first page—it is the figure of Samson that dominates throughout, a domination that is shared only with St Edmund. Jocelin appears to have been a local man, and has been associated with the quarter of the town called Brakelond. He entered the monastery in 1173, probably after attending the monastic school. Samson was then the novice master, and Jocelin became much subjected to him. By 1180 Jocelin had been made chaplain to the prior, who, on Abbot Hugh's death in that year, became temporary head of the convent. When Samson was elected abbot in 1182, Jocelin was appointed his chaplain and was with the abbot 'day and night' for six years.

Jocelin is a gifted writer, almost a diarist and in part a biographer. Because of his sheer quality as a writer, his observation, sensitivity, and discrimination, we enter the inner life of the monks and the community. World-shaking events, wars, and political manœuvrings are recorded, but Jocelin pays greatest attention to what went on within the

community and within men's minds. His views of men and
events change—he almost bares his soul, he does not
conceal his personal disappointments. It is very much a
personal story, but it is also a unique insight into the
anatomy of medieval society. Three figures dominate this
book: Edmund (the royal Saint), Samson (the abbot), and
Jocelin himself (the monk). We must start with St Edmund.

Of overriding importance to the life of the community at
Bury was St Edmund, king of the East Angles, martyred
by the Danes in 869—when he was shot with arrows and
beheaded—whose continuing presence was felt by the
monks of his house centuries after his death. The monks
saw themselves as St Edmund's men, almost as his fighting
host. St Edmund protected them: they in turn safeguarded
his rights and name. Their commitment was both personal
and intensely local and partisan. Samson's dream as a child,
which Jocelin narrates, illustrates the force and power of St
Edmund in the minds of the people of Norfolk and Suffolk.
Sweyn, father of King Cnut, had been struck dead at St
Edmund's tomb in 1014 for threatening to destroy the
Saint's town of Bury unless he was paid a large ransom. By
Jocelin's time, there were paintings of this dramatic scene
near St Edmund's shrine. The power of the Saint had also
been displayed in the mid-eleventh century when he para-
lysed the hands of Abbot Leofstan, who had pulled the
Saint's head to see whether it had been miraculously united
with the body. In 1163, ten years before Jocelin entered the
community, Henry of Essex, a successful and influential
nobleman, was defeated in a duel owing to the supernatural
power of the Saint. Jocelin repeats this story. From the
moment of entering the monastery, if not before, the
novices became acquainted with the details of St Edmund's
life and martyrdom. These had been written down by Abbo
of Fleury in the late tenth century, and formed the basis of
the tradition in which Jocelin and others were brought up.

The abbey church was St Edmund's house, and he the

intercessor between the fraternity and the distant figure of God. Behind the high altar in a prominent site, stood from 1095 the shrine of St Edmund. Flanked by the entombed relics of two seventh-century saints, St Jurmin, son of King Anna of the East Angles, and St Botolph, it provided the focus of an East Anglian royal cult. Already honoured by Kings Cnut and Edward the Confessor, St Edmund's cult was further promoted by William the Conqueror and his successors.

Building and beautifying a worthy domicile for the Saint was a sacred charge. The Romanesque church begun by Abbot Baldwin (1065–97) was one of the most splendid in Europe. Over 500 feet in length (50 feet longer than the cathedral at Norwich), it had an apsidal east end with an ambulatory and radiating chapels, transepts, and a large western narthex to allow the flow of pilgrims to assemble and circulate. Baldwin had been a monk of St Denis near Paris, and the great European pilgrimage churches doubtless influenced his plans. Under Abbot Anselm, an Italian (1120–48), who had been a monk of St Saba, Rome, the west front was completed. This front had been inspired by Alexander the Magnificent's west front at Lincoln with its three deep recesses, and in turn influenced that of Peterborough abbey (1193–1200). It had bronze doors—as survive in many important Italian churches, for example, at Pisa and Verona—which were the work of an Italian artist, Master Hugo, no doubt engaged by Anselm. The most imposing building left today, the gateway tower of St James, which housed the bells, and through which Samson passed to his installation, was also constructed under Abbot Anselm. The west front as remodelled by Abbot Samson was very broad, 246 feet across, and was capped with twin octagonal towers and surmounted in the centre by a huge western tower. The pages of Jocelin record Samson's burning desire, both as sacrist and as abbot, to complete the towers of the abbey church. For this he used some of the oaks at Elmset, in Long Melford, about which Jocelin tells an amusing story, for Geoffrey Ridel, bishop of Ely, had cast envious eyes on them. When finished, the abbey's western front very probably bore some resemblance to that of Ely, erected at almost the same time, whose splendour we can still contemplate.

Of the shrine of St Edmund we have no clear visual evidence, but it probably looked much like that of St Osmund at Salisbury (which has survived) and that of St Thomas Becket, which is depicted in the 'miracle' glass at Canterbury, with its two large 'port-holes' through which pilgrims might insert their bodies, supervised by the wardens of the shrine. From Jocelin's description of the fire we know that St Edmund's shrine was formed of gold plates, decorated with coloured stones. A canopy, which was commissioned by Abbot Samson, surmounted the structure. To this tomb fled those in trouble, seeking the protection of the Saint. Samson, before he became a monk, apprehensive that his mission to Rome on behalf of the abbey had failed and that he would incur the displeasure of the abbot, sought refuge under the shrine. Fearing the abbot, no layman dared to bring him food openly nor the monks to speak to him, but neither did anyone dare to drag him out for fear of St Edmund, for the holy area round the shrine acted as a sanctuary. To the shrine, too, came pilgrims in search of miraculous cures. Bury, with Canterbury after 1170 and Walsingham by the end of the fourteenth century, was one of the main English centres of pilgrimage, outstripped by the other two later, but in Jocelin's time a flourishing centre of more than local fame. Places of miraculous cure attracted doctors as well as sufferers, and Bury from the time of Abbot Baldwin, who had been royal physician to Edward the Confessor, William I, and William II, numbered monks with medical training in its community. Amongst those chosen by Abbot Samson to witness the opening of St Edmund's tomb after the fire was Walter the physician, the monastery's almoner, who had made money out of medical fees taken from a private practice. After inspection, the incorrupt body was carefully returned to its resting place amid protestations that in future the shrine would be better cared for.

The medieval idea of power centred, naturally enough, on those who exercised it—the saint, the priest, the lay ruler, through whom God worked. All in authority ultimately received their powers from God. Power came from above: the hierarchical descent of its exercise flowed through the lawfully elected pope, who, as the vicar of St Peter, represented the 'prince' of the Apostles on earth. The pope had a singular significance for both lay rulers and ecclesiastics and, indeed, for all men. His existence and activities affected the life of every person. As St Peter's representative (later, it was argued, as Christ's vicar), the pope had the moral and spiritual power to declare how society should be ordered and how its resources should be used to further the Christian faith.

The abbey of Bury had two powerful protectors—the pope and the Crown. Already before the Norman Conquest, a political power-base had been established for the abbot in West Suffolk. For the confirmation and upholding of its political rights the abbey turned naturally to the king. For the confirmation of its status as a major ecclesiastical community that housed the body of one of Christ's saints, it looked to the pope. Certain great monastic houses, such as Bury, sought exemption from the jurisdiction of the diocesan bishop and the archbishop. They sought, too, the symbols of this authority, the right for the abbot to wear the pontificals: mitre, ring, tunic, dalmatic, sandals, and gloves. During the course of the late twelfth century, when Jocelin was writing, Bury achieved exemption (and other privileges that only a pope could grant) by dint of frequent petitions and visits to the pope. Although the area that came to be declared exempt from the bishop's supervision was not very large at Bury (about the mile encircling the town), the abbot achieved for his community exemption from visitation both by the diocesan, the bishop of Norwich, and the provincial, the archbishop of Canterbury. The right of visitation meant that the visitor could enter the particular abbey or religious establishment, summon the monks to the chapter-house, and enquire into all aspects of their life and administration of affairs. As a result of his investigations, he could issue injunctions which he could enforce under threat of sentences of suspension from priestly office, excommunication from the sacraments of the church, and interdict (decrees against celebrating services). By the mid twelfth century the archbishops of Canterbury acquired from the pope the title of legate, and hence had further powers to visit as the pope's representative. Jealous of its rights and position, Bury put up a spirited fight against archbishops and legates—Richard of Dover, William de Longchamps, Hubert Walter—exercising any powers over the monastery. The privileges which Bury acquired were accounted for by papal favour, but were buttressed by the abbey's great temporal powers and standing with the Crown.

The landed endowment that had been given to St Edmund's church in the mid tenth century was greatly enlarged by Edward the Confessor, who gave to the abbot of St Edmund's jurisdictional and administrative powers over the 'eight and a half hundreds' that came to form West Suffolk and to be known as the 'Liberty of St Edmund'. Royal government in the English localities operated through subdivisions of counties, called 'hundreds', each having judicial, fiscal, and administrative functions, subject to the king's chief official in each shire, the sheriff. In the Liberty of St Edmund, however, the abbot acted as the king's representative, and the sheriff of Suffolk had no power. Every aspect of royal government had to go through the abbot and his agents—whether it was the execution of royal writs, the collection of royal taxation, or the administration of royal justice. Even serious criminal cases, the 'pleas of the Crown', which were normally reserved for judgement by the king's judges, belonged to the abbot. The abbot's 'great court of pleas' at Bury was the Liberty's equivalent of the king's county court, and within the hundreds the hundredal courts, meeting every three weeks, sat under the presidency of the abbot's bailiff, who collected taxes, fines, and other dues on behalf of both king and abbot. At several points in Jocelin's *Chronicle*, Abbot Samson is heard insisting on the importance of his responsibility to administer royal justice. Failure to do so might have the disastrous consequence of provoking the king to step in, thus depriving the glorious martyr St Edmund of his rights. Samson sometimes speaks as if St Edmund died in order to win these rights. This is the indignant spirit in which the abbot faced attempts by certain landholders, such as the monks of Canterbury and of Ely, to undermine St Edmund's authority within the Liberty.

Whereas the Liberty was an area of jurisdiction, including both manors belonging to the abbey and manors held by other landowners, the 'Barony of St Edmund' consisted of the abbey's own estates, both inside and outside the Liberty. By 1066 Bury's estates stretched through several counties, though they were chiefly in Suffolk. Like all other great property owners, the abbot was required, from the time of William the Conqueror, to provide a certain number of knights to serve in the king's army. This baronial obligation brought the abbot into the royal circle as one of the chief men of the kingdom, to be consulted on great matters of state. Another consequence of baronial status was that on the abbot's death, the Barony passed into royal custody until a successor was elected, in the same way that the estates of an heir who was under age passed into his lord's wardship.

The feudal quota due from the Barony of St Edmund

was forty knights, and like any other baron, the abbot established tenants in his estates, who in return for their lands, called 'fees', were obliged to perform knight-service when required. This consisted of forty days' duties at their own expense each year—active campaigning in wartime and guard duty at the royal castle of Norwich in peace. Frequently the service was compounded for a money payment, known as 'scutage'. By the late twelfth century, the system was subject to various strains: among them the escalating cost of knighthood, the reluctance of knights to serve overseas, and the complications produced by the tendency for barons to 'enfeoff' more knights than they owed to the king. In the Barony of St Edmund, which owed forty knights, there were fifty fees: Samson's chief dispute with his knights was over the extra ten knights' service claimed by him and denied by them.

The chief function of the estates of St Edmund, however, was to provide for the upkeep of the monastery and its community. A large number of the best manors were not granted out as knights' fees but retained for more direct exploitation: these were the 'demesne' manors. A division was made very early in the twelfth century between the manors assigned to the abbot of Bury and those belonging to the convent. They were administered separately, the convent's manors not forming part of the Barony that would pass into the king's custody during vacancies. Before Samson's time the demesnes were commonly leased out for fixed cash payments. This system simplified the administration, but had great disadvantages in a period of rapid inflation, such as the later twelfth century, and doubtless contributed to the acute financial problems that caused Samson's immediate predecessor, Abbot Hugh, to contract large loans from moneylenders. Jocelin describes Samson's solution of taking the demesne manors back into direct management, to be run by bailiffs who were responsible to him for all manorial income and expenditure. Samson also reverted to the older practice of travelling from manor to manor, both to supervise the bailiffs and to save expense by living off the produce of his estates and the food-rents paid by the peasantry. Sometimes, however, it was not easy to distinguish between manors held as knights' fees and demesne manors held on leases, which might be called 'fee farms'. Men who had held both kinds of tenancy for many years, and whose families had been in possession for two or three generations, might well claim hereditary right in lands which had originally been granted on leases: this was the difficulty at the heart of Abbot Samson's dispute with the Cockfield family.

Lordship over land usually involved lordship over the churches on the land. The abbot and convent possessed the churches of their own manors, and also acquired others from gifts by other manorial lords, in all totalling sixty-five parish churches. Patronage, or 'advowson', of a church brought several benefits. The right to appoint the incumbent enabled the abbot or convent to reward members of the clergy who were useful as clerks, legal representatives, and envoys. Hence the long struggle over the church of Woolpit. In economic terms, control over a parish church was also a source of income, bringing with it the greater part of the tithes (renders of 10 per cent of all the villagers' produce) and other ecclesiastical taxes. When, as a New Year present for Abbot Samson, Jocelin composed his list of the abbot's thirty-six churches and the convent's twenty-nine, he carefully added the estimated value of every church. By far the richest of all was the abbot's church of Long Melford, at £40—an income that would have hired a trained knight, with horse, equipment, and squire, for a whole year.

St Edmund's town of Beodricsworth, to which his body was brought in the early 900s, belonged to the monks of Bury, and formed no part of the abbot's Barony. Edward the Confessor granted a mint, and its currency bears the first use of the name, 'St Edmund's Bury'. (Bury, from *burh*, means a fortified town.) The town grew in importance with the convent. Under Abbot Baldwin (1065–97) five new streets were constructed to the west of the abbey, running from north to south on a grid plan, still clearly visible in aerial views. Baldwin also provided a new market-place, which was crucial to the town's future prosperity, and constructed some further 342 houses, so that by the time of Domesday Book (1086), the town had about 500 dwellings. Many of the inhabitants gained a living from the monks. Domesday Book speaks of seventy-five bakers, ale-brewers, tailors, washerwomen, shoemakers, robemakers, cooks, porters, and purveyors, who 'daily wait upon the Saint, the abbot, and the brethren'. By the thirteenth century, when there were eighty monks in the monastery, there were 111 servants who lived in, and very many more domiciled in the town.

The town's arable land lay in the West, South, and East fields, where, alongside the townsmen's holdings, the convent had 400 acres. But the town's real financial importance to the convent was not in agricultural produce but in urban property—in the house rents, market dues, and tolls. The owners of the burgage tenements—often basically work-shops with living accommodation over—were free men. As such they could leave their properties by will or dispose of them by sale. They paid certain rents and other payments to the monks, but otherwise they were free to determine their lives and to run their businesses much as they would. The residents of the *banleuca* (the surrounding area or suburb) did not have the privileges of those who dwelt within the walls, but they did have more freedom than country dwellers. The monastic officer, the sacrist, con-trolled the borough court and appointed the town reeves, or bailiffs. He was thus responsible for the administration of justice, and had a gaol. The monks remained the overlords of the town until the abbey was dissolved in 1539, but the burgesses began much earlier to seek more self-government.

Within the town of Bury a Jewish quarter had emerged by the time of Jocelin. The Jewish community flourished on the convent of Bury's difficulties in raising cash or ready money, but there were on the whole good relations and trust between creditor and debtor. Jews roamed the great church, as Jocelin says, and during the troubles of 1173–4 their wives and children were given shelter within one of the conventual buildings. Growing economic rivalry, however, increased tensions between Jews and Christians. To this period belongs the stone house, called Moyses Hall, associated with Jewish wealth. In 1181 a Christian boy, Robert, was alleged to have been 'ritually' murdered by Jews—he was immediately venerated in the abbey—and after the riots of Palm Sunday 1190, in which fifty-seven Jews were killed, Abbot Samson expelled the Jewish community from the town. Jocelin regards Samson's action as a sign of the abbot's 'greatness', to be classed with such deeds as his foundation of the hospital at Babwell, repurchase of the manor of Mildenhall, and refurbishment of St Edmund's shrine. The Saint's town was no longer to be a haven for those who were not St Edmund's men.

Over the *Chronicle* towers the enigmatic figure of Samson. The abbot is God's tool and representative. The source of his authority lies in the sixth-century Rule of St Benedict which describes the abbot as 'holding the place of Christ' in the monastery, and as the father (or *Abba*) of the community. For his family or flock, the abbot is responsible and answerable to God. At this time the image of the father, like the image of God, was both loving and stern, evoking both affectionate and fearful responses. In Jocelin's account, Samson's care and concern for his monks and his church have a dark side: in order to bring about the best, Samson is frequently angry, even savage. Like the biblical Samson, he had a violent nature. Before he was elected

abbot, some of the monks had dreams about his appointment: one saw him as a fighter, ready to strike, and another
was told by a prophet that Samson would 'rage like a wolf'.
As abbot, his authority was immense: through his court he
had the power of life and death over the inhabitants of West
Suffolk, and within the abbey he had the power to excommunicate, imprison, or inflict corporal punishment on the
monks. Understandably, fear of the abbot is an emotion
that surfaces frequently in Jocelin's narrative.

The first duty of the monk was obedience to the abbot
'without delay', and his goal was the salvation of his soul,
to be achieved with the help of the novice master and of
the abbot. The monk's day was filled with the round of
communal prayer. Each week the whole of the Psalter was
recited. Within each year the greater part of the Bible was
read, and every day a section of the Rule, so that the monks
came to hear it in entirety three times a year. Outside the
daily services in the choir and the meeting of the community
in the chapter-house, the monks attended to the study of
scriptural texts and holy works in the cloister. Although the
day was theoretically divided into prayer, study, and physical work, by the 1170s the amount of time spent on
agricultural and manual labour was minimal. The small,
self-supporting communities of early times had come, by
the late twelfth century, to be wealthy and influential
corporations with vast landed estates requiring administrators. These were recruited from amongst the monks themselves. The growth of the 'obedientiary' system produced
monks who spent no time at all in the cloister but dedicated
the major part of their activities, outside choir and chapter,
to the running of the domestic and external affairs of the
convent. Such men came to control separate households
within the monastery and to have their own incomes and
servants, to raise their own loans (often from the Jews), and
to wield very considerable jurisdictional powers.

Foremost among the obedientiaries at Bury were the

cellarer and the sacrist. From his offices in the great north court, the cellarer was responsible for most of the abbey's manors, including the convent's manor within the town of Bury of which he was lord, controlling all the mills and sheepfolds, taking tolls, and buying first in the market. His job was to see to the provision of food and drink for the convent. During the abbot's absences—which were frequent at the beginning of Samson's rule—the cellarer had to entertain the abbot's guests: this led to friction and dispute about shouldering the cost. The sacrist, whose house and workshops were in the south court, was concerned—as were sacrists at other abbeys—with maintaining the fabric of the church and conventual buildings. At Bury, however, the sacrist had additional duties and powers, for he was lord of the borough of St Edmund, and so held a court for the town and the *banleuca*. The other obedientiaries at Bury were less influential. Jocelin mentions the almoner, who dealt with the charitable activities of the convent, and some of the others, such as the wardens of St Edmund's shrine, the chamberlain, who looked after the monks' clothing, and the guest-master (an office he held himself), but the most conspicuous are clearly the cellarer and the sacrist. Throughout the course of Jocelin's narrative the tensions are subtly described between these worldly businessmen, some of them of little education, and the more contemplative and intellectual monks in the convent, men who filled the offices of importance in the cloister: the novice master, and the second and third priors who saw to the discipline of the monks.

Although the monks of Bury had many strong links with the outside world, and lived in close association with laymen and seculars, yet for part of their days, at least, they formed an exclusive and separate community. This close brotherhood, however, was not free of internal tension and conflict. There were differences of opinion and clashes of personality. The obedientiary system itself probably provided more opportunity for rivalry than for co-operation, particularly between the cellarer and the sacrist, and may well have encouraged ambition, greed, and jealousy. Among the monks there were alliances and divisions of various sorts: the juniors against the seniors, the ignorant against the learned, the cloister monks against the obedientiaries. Jocelin does not hide these and other dissensions, and reveals frequent grumblings and complaints against the abbot. Complaints and criticism are expressly forbidden several times in the Rule, as being contrary to the all-important principle of obedience. In the most scandalous incident, when the rebellious mutterings became a positive uproar, the conflict between abbot and convent was so serious that Samson believed the monks were conspiring to murder him. Finally a tearful reconciliation took place, although its terms were not entirely satisfactory to the disaffected monks. In such an atmosphere of strong emotions, there were some 'particular friendships' between monks: Jocelin describes one of his own friendships, and how it came to an end through his tactlessness. It is this honesty, coupled with human wisdom and understanding, that makes Jocelin's *Chronicle* perennially attractive, a 'classic', as that great man of letters, Thomas Carlyle, realized.

NOTE ON TEXT AND TRANSLATION

THE LATIN TEXT used for this translation is that of the Nelson's Medieval Classics, *The Chronicle of Jocelin of Brakelond*, with a parallel translation by H. E. Butler, published in 1949. It is based on the only complete manuscript, British Library Harley MS 1005, which dates from the mid to late thirteenth century. For notes on this manuscript, and on three others that give copies of parts of the chronicle, see Sir Roger Mynors' comments in the Nelson edition, pp. xi–xiii. Our collation of the printed text with the manuscripts has revealed a few trifling corrections, of which we have taken account in our translation.

We have attempted in our translation to reproduce the essential simplicity and straightforwardness of Jocelin's style and the easy flow of his narrative, but we have divided the chronicle into chapters, for which we have supplied headings, in order to facilitate its use by modern readers. Any other words added by us for the sake of clarity are shown in square brackets: these are chiefly identifications of persons, places, dates, and quotations. Places named are all in Suffolk unless otherwise noted. Like most medieval writers, Jocelin employed quotations and allusions throughout his work. We have given the sources of direct quotations, but have not signalled the many occasions on which Jocelin simply alludes to or echoes other works. Over two-thirds of his quotations are from the Vulgate Bible, chiefly from the Psalms and the Gospels. Most of the remaining quotations are taken from classical authors, among whom the best represented are Ovid and Horace.

We have reproduced sums of money in the form in which they occur in Jocelin's text. The only coins minted were silver pennies. 12 pennies (12*d*.) = 1 shilling (1*s*.); 20*s*. = £1. The mark was a measure of weight, two-thirds of £1. 1 mark = 13*s*. 4*d*.; 3 marks = £2.

SELECT BIBLIOGRAPHY

GENERAL WORKS

ON the CHURCH and PAPACY, the two most significant books of recent times are R. W. Southern, *Western Society and the Church in the Middle Ages* (Pelican History of the Church 2, 1970) and W. Ullmann, *A Short History of the Papacy in the Middle Ages* (Methuen, 1972; UP, 1974). Both are individual interpretations by great scholars: in our view they give by far the best picture of the importance of ecclesiastical institutions in medieval life. For the 1,400th anniversary of the death of St Benedict, the founder of Western monasticism, exhibitions were held throughout Europe. On this occasion, for its own exhibition, the British Library published *The Benedictines in Britain* (British Library. Series no. 3, 1980), a valuable survey of the Benedictines' contribution to British society. C. H. Lawrence's *Medieval Monasticism* (Longman, 1984) gives an account of the development of the orders. However, no serious student can afford to neglect Dom David Knowles' *The Monastic Order in England* (Cambridge, 2nd edn., 1963), a work which is as readable as it is illuminating. Recently there has been a renewed interest among historians in the meaning of miracles and pilgrimages in medieval life. Representative of this trend are Ronald C. Finucane, *Miracles and Pilgrims. Popular Beliefs in Medieval England* (Dent, 1977), and Jonathan Sumption, *Pilgrimage. An Image of Mediaeval Religion* (Faber & Faber, 1975).

On GOVERNMENT, KINGSHIP, and the ARISTOCRACY, D. M. Stenton's *English Society in the Early Middle Ages (1066–1307)* (Pelican History of England 3, 4th edn. 1965, repr. 1985) and A. L. Poole's *From Domesday Book to Magna Carta* (2nd edn., Oxford, 1955) remain the two best outline accounts. A newer study, based on more recent research is W. L. Warren, *The Governance of Norman and Angevin England 1086–1272* (Arnold, 1987). M. T. Clanchy's *England and its Rulers 1066–1272* (Fontana Paperbacks, 1983) is concerned with the impact of Norman and

French influences on English society. Three important biographical studies of English kings in the period are: W. L. Warren, *Henry II* (Eyre Methuen, 1973); John Gillingham, *Richard the Lionheart* (Weidenfeld, 1978); W. L. Warren, *King John* (Penguin, 1961). Maurice Keen's *Chivalry* (Yale UP, 1984) explores the aristocratic ideals of knighthood.

TOWNS, RURAL SOCIETY, and THE ECONOMY: Colin Platt, *The English Medieval Town* (Secker & Warburg, 1986) is a readable and well-illustrated introduction, while E. Miller and J. Hatcher, *Medieval England: Rural Society and Economic Change 1086–1348* (Longman, 1978), is a study of agrarian development.

LITERATURE and ART: On the literature written in the English language, J. A. Burrow, *Medieval Writers and their Work. Middle English Literature and its Background 1100–1500* (Oxford paperback, 1982) is a helpful guide. On art T. S. R. Boase's *English Art 1100–1216* (Oxford History of English Art, 1953) covers all branches of art and architecture: no recent work is so comprehensive.

SPECIFIC WORKS ON BURY ST EDMUNDS

The Town

M. W. Beresford and J. K. S. St Joseph, *Medieval England. An Aerial Survey* (Cambridge, 2nd edn. 1979), 215–17 and fig. 91, and see J. T. Smith, 'A note on the origin of the town-plan of Bury St Edmunds', *Archaeological Journal*, cviii (1952), 162–4. M. D. Lobel, *The Borough of Bury St Edmund's. A Study in the Government and Development of a Monastic Town* (Oxford, 1935) is out of print, but has not been superseded.

The Abbey

A. B. Whittingham, *Bury St Edmunds Abbey* (Department of the Environment, HMSO, 1976: now out of print) is a revised and shortened version of his article in *Archaeological Journal*, 108 (1952), 168–87. Particularly useful is R. Gilyard-Beer, 'The eastern arm of the abbey church at Bury St Edmund', *Proceedings of the Suffolk Institute of Archaeology*, 31 (1967–9), 256–62, who deals with the excavations of 1957–64 after the site passed to the

Ministry of Works. See also David Knowles and J. K. S. St Joseph, *Monastic Sites from the Air* (Cambridge, 1952), 14–15.

The Liberty

The immense powers of the abbot of Bury in the government of West Suffolk are discussed by H. M. Cam, 'The King's government, as administered by the greater abbots of East Anglia', in *Liberties and Communities in Medieval England* (1963).

Sources

For source material to which Jocelin refers, see *The Rule of Saint Benedict in Latin and English*, ed. and trans. Abbot Justin McCann (1952), and *English Historical Documents*, ii. *1042–1189*, ed. D. C. Douglas and G. W. Greenaway, 2nd edn. (1981), and iii. *1189–1327*, ed. H. Rothwell (1975). Much of Bury's rich and important archive has been put into print in the last hundred years: *Memorials of St Edmund's Abbey*, ed. T. Arnold, 3 vols. (Rolls Series, 1890–6) includes a Latin text of Jocelin's chronicle (now superseded by the Nelson edition) together with several other Bury chronicles; *The Kalendar of Abbot Samson of Bury St Edmunds and Related Documents*, ed. R. H. C. Davis (Camden 3rd series 84, 1954); and *Feudal Documents from the Abbey of Bury St Edmund's*, ed. D. C. Douglas (British Academy, 1932). R. M. Thomson, *The Archives of the Abbey of Bury St Edmunds* (Suffolk Record Society 21, 1980), lists the surviving records of the house.

A CHRONOLOGY OF
JOCELIN'S NARRATIVE

1193	Second visit of Longchamps to Bury, pp. 47–8. Samson present at siege of Windsor; visits the king in Germany and returns, pp. 49, 69
1194	Release and return of King Richard I, p. 49
1195	Illegal tournament held near Bury, p. 50
1195–7	Archbishop Hubert Walter attempts legatine visitation of Bury, pp. 72–5
1196	Pope Celestine III forbids Archbishop Hubert Walter to conduct visitation of Bury, p. 74
1196–7	Samson's dispute and settlement with his knights over castle-guard service, pp. 58–60. Dispute with the London merchants over tolls in Bury market, pp. 67–8
1197	Samson visits the king in Normandy to settle dispute over his knights' refusal to serve outside England, pp. 76–7. Samson's appointment of his clerk to supervise the cellarer, pp. 77–81
1197–8	Samson visits Oxford and Coventry, pp. 83–4
1198	Innocent III elected pope, p. 87. Fire at St Edmund's shrine; Samson opens the tomb, pp. 94–102
1199	Death of King Richard I; accession of King John, who visits Bury, pp. 102–3
1200	Survey of knights' fees, pp. 106–8
1201	Abbots of Cluny and Chertsey visit Bury, p. 110. Cockfield case heard before the king's court, pp. 109–10. Death of Prior Robert; appointment of Prior Herbert, pp. 110–15. Abbot of Flay visits Bury, p. 117. Monks of Ely set up a market at Lakenheath, pp. 117–19
1201–2	Samson's disputes with bishop of Ely over jurisdiction, p. 119, and with monks of Bury over their rights, pp. 120–2
?1202	Death of Jocelin of Brakelond

Chronicle of the
Abbey of Bury St Edmunds

The Abbey in debt

I HAVE been concerned here to record what I know from personal experience of the events that took place in St Edmund's church in my time, describing the bad deeds as well as the good, to provide both warning and example. I begin in the year in which the Flemings were taken prisoner outside the town [1173]:* that was the year in which I entered the monastery and Prior Hugh was deposed and Robert appointed in his place. By then Abbot Hugh had grown old and was losing his sight.* A gentle and kind man, he was a good and devout monk, but lacked ability in business matters. He was too dependent on those around him and too ready to believe them, relying more on the opinions of others than on his own judgement. Although discipline, worship and everything connected with the Rule flourished within the cloister, external affairs were badly managed. Every employee, seeing that the abbot was naïve and elderly, ignored his duty and did as he pleased. The abbot's villages and all the hundreds were leased out, the woodlands were destroyed, the manorial houses were about to collapse, and from day to day everything grew steadily worse. The abbot sought refuge and consolation in a single remedy: that of borrowing money, to maintain at least the dignity of his household. In the last eight years of his life [1173–80], sums of £100 or £200 were regularly added to the debt every Easter and Michaelmas. The bonds were always renewed, and further loans were taken out to pay the growing interest.

This infection spread, from the top downwards, from the ruler to the ruled, so that before long each obedientiary had his own seal and pledged himself in debt as he chose, to both Jews and Christians. Silk copes, gold vessels, and other church ornaments were often pawned without the consent of the convent. I saw a bond made out to William son of Isabel,* for £1,040, and another to Isaac son of Rabbi Joce,* for £40, but I never discovered what lay behind these transactions. However, I do know the full story relating to a third bond that I saw, in favour of Benedict the Jew of Norwich,* for £880. Our treasury building was in a dilapidated condition, and William the sacrist was determined to restore it, come what may. He secretly borrowed 40 marks at interest from Benedict the Jew, to whom he gave a bond sealed with the seal that used to hang on the shrine of St Edmund and was normally used for sealing documents of guilds and fraternities. Afterwards, but too late, this seal was destroyed by order of the convent. When the sum owed had risen to £100, the Jew arrived with a letter from the king* concerning the sacrist's debt, and in this way the secret was revealed to the abbot and convent. The abbot was furious, and would have deposed the sacrist, claiming that he had authority from the pope to dismiss him when he wished. But someone went to the abbot, and speaking on the sacrist's behalf, so deceived him that he allowed another bond to be made out for Benedict the Jew, this time for £400 to be paid at the end of four years. This was for the £100 already accumulated at interest and another £100 which the Jew lent the sacrist for the abbot's use. The sacrist undertook in full chapter to repay the whole debt, and a bond was drawn up which was sealed with the conventual seal, because the abbot would not use his own, pretending that the debt was not his affair. Four years later [?1177], when the obligation could not be met, a new bond was issued, for £880 to be paid off at fixed terms, at £80 per annum. The same Jew held several other bonds for smaller debts and one that was for fourteen years, so that altogether he was owed £1,200, excluding the compound interest.

Talk of these large debts reached the king, as R., the king's almoner,* told the abbot when he came on a visit.

After the abbot had consulted the prior and a few others, the almoner was conducted into the chapter-house, and while we sat in silence, the abbot said, 'Here is the king's almoner, our lord and friend, who out of love for God and St Edmund, has informed me that the king has received an unfavourable report about us, to the effect that the affairs of the church are being mismanaged both inside the convent and outside. Therefore I command you in obedience to speak up honestly and openly about the present situation here.' [Robert] the prior rose to speak as representative of all. He said that the church was in good order, that the Rule was very scrupulously observed within the convent, and that although, like some of our neighbours, we had run up a few small debts, our business was being conducted ably and wisely, and no debt would cause us any trouble. Hearing this, the king's almoner replied that he was very glad to have this authoritative account from the convent, or rather, from the prior.

On another occasion [between April 1174 and April 1175], when Archbishop Richard came into our chapter as papal legate (before we had our present exemption),* the prior, and with him Master Geoffrey de Constantino,* said just the same, defending the abbot. At that time I was a novice, in the care of Master Samson, later abbot, who taught me the Rule. As soon as I had the chance, I asked him, 'What are these rumours? Why do you remain silent when you know perfectly well what is going on—you a cloister monk, who is not ambitious for office and fears God more than man?' Samson replied, 'My son, a child who has recently been burned is afraid of fire: that is how it is with me and many others. Prior Hugh has recently been deposed and sent into exile. Denis and H[ugh] and R[oger] of Ingham* have only lately come back from exile. Like them, I was imprisoned and then sent to Acre [Castle Acre, Norf.],* because we spoke out for the good of our church against the abbot's wishes. This is the hour of darkness.

This is the hour in which flatterers prevail and are believed:
their might is increased and we can do nothing against it.
For the time being we must ignore these things. Let the
Lord look down and judge.'

News reached Abbot Hugh that Archbishop Richard of
Canterbury wished to come and make an inspection of our
church, in his capacity as papal legate. After the abbot had
taken advice, he sent off to Rome to obtain exemption from
the legate's authority. When the messenger came back from
Rome [1175], there was nothing with which to pay the sums
he had promised to the pope and cardinals, except, in the
special circumstances, the cross over the high altar, and the
two images which Archbishop Stigand had beautified with
a great weight of gold and silver and had given to St
Edmund—the 'Mariola' and the 'John'.* Some of our
monks who were particularly close to the abbot said that to
pay for such an important exemption the precious metal
ought to be stripped off the shrine of St Edmund itself.
They did not perceive the dangerous potential of the
privilege: that if any abbot should choose to run down the
church's possessions and misgovern his convent, there
would be no one to whom the community could complain
concerning his misdeeds, for he would fear no bishop,
archbishop, or legate, and his immunity from punishment
would encourage him in wrongdoing.

At that time the cellarer, like the other officials, borrowed
money from Jurnet the Jew,* without consulting the convent, in a bond sealed with the seal I mentioned previously.
But when the debt had grown to £60, the convent was
summoned to pay the cellarer's debt. He was deposed,
although he alleged that on the abbot's orders he had for
the last three years entertained in the guest-house, whether
the abbot was at home or not, all those guests who,
according to abbey custom, ought to have been entertained
by the abbot himself. Master Denis* replaced him, and by
careful management brought the debt of £60 down to £30.

Towards this we paid the 30 marks that the convent received from Benedict of Blakenham for a lease of the manors of Nowton and Whepstead. But still to this day the Jew retains a bond for £26 capital and the cellarer's debt.

Two days after Master Denis became cellarer, three knights with their esquires were brought into the guesthouse to be entertained there, although the abbot was at home and in his lodgings. When that high-minded Achilles heard this, not wishing to fail in his office as others had done, he sprang up, and taking the keys of the cellary with him, escorted the knights into the abbot's hall, and went to the abbot and said, 'Father, you are well aware that it is the abbey custom that knights and laymen are received in the abbot's house, if he is at home. I cannot and will not entertain your guests. If you cannot accept this, take back the keys of the cellary and appoint another cellarer as you think fit.' When the abbot heard this he received those knights whether he liked it or not, and ever afterwards accommodated knights and laymen according to the ancient custom. They are still so received when the abbot is at home.

At one time the abbot wished to win the favour of Master Samson and appointed him subsacrist. Samson was frequently criticized, and was often transferred from one office to another: he was made guest-master, then pittancer,* then third prior, and then subsacrist again. Many opposed him in those days, though later they became his flatterers. But he, unlike the other officials, never succumbed to flattery, and for this reason the abbot used to tell his close friends that Samson the subsacrist was the only man he had ever known who could not be bent to his will.

Abbot Hugh's death 1180

IN the twenty-third year of his abbacy [1180], the abbot decided to go to pray at the shrine of St Thomas [Becket,

at Canterbury]. On the way there, he had a bad fall from
his horse near Rochester on 9 September: his kneecap was
dislocated and lodged itself at the back of his knee. Doctors
hurried to him, but although they put him through many
torments, they did not cure him. He was carried back here
in a horse-litter, and devotedly cared for, as was proper.
There is not much more to tell, for his leg festered and the
illness affected his heart: a tertian fever set in and he died
during its fourth attack, giving up his soul to God on the
day after the Feast of St Brice [14 November 1180].

But before he was dead, everything was stolen by his
servants: not a thing was left in the abbot's house except
three-legged stools and tables that could not be carried
away. There remained over his body only a coverlet and
two old torn blankets with which someone had replaced the
whole ones they had taken. There was not a pennyworth
left to be given to the poor for the good of his soul.
[William] the sacrist said that it was not his business to see
to it, as he had found the expenses for the abbot and his
household for a whole month, because the tenant-farmers
refused to give anything before the proper rent day, and
the creditors would not lend anything, realizing that the
abbot was fatally ill. However, [Richard] the tenant of
Palgrave produced 50s. for distribution to the poor, because
he entered into his tenancy on that very day. But those 50s.
were later surrendered to the king's bailiffs, who demanded
the full rent for the king.

After the abbot's funeral, it was resolved in chapter that
the news of his death should be reported to Ranulph de
Glanville, justiciar of England.* With all speed Master
Samson and Master R. Ruffus, monks of our house, crossed
the Channel to inform the king.* They obtained royal
letters stating that the property and revenues of the convent, which were separate from those of the abbot, should
be entirely in the control of the prior and convent, while
the rest of the abbey should be in the king's hands. The

custody of the abbot's property was granted to Robert of Cockfield and the steward Robert de Flamville,* who immediately took securities* from all the members of the abbot's household and kindred to whom he had made any gifts during his last illness, and from those who had taken away any of the abbot's belongings. These included even the abbot's chaplain, one of our monks, for whom the prior stood surety. The custodians also entered our vestry and made an inventory in duplicate of all the ornaments of the church.

The vacancy 1180–1182—Samson as subsacrist

WHILE there was no abbot, [Robert] the prior concentrated all his attention on preserving tranquillity within the convent and upholding our church's reputation for hospitality towards guests. His aim was to keep everybody and everything on an even keel by not upsetting or angering anyone. Nevertheless, he chose to ignore faults that ought to have been corrected in the conduct of the obedientiaries. This was especially true in the case of [William] the sacrist, who behaved during the vacancy as though he did not care what he did with his department, neither paying any debts nor putting up any buildings, yet foolishly squandering income from offerings and gifts. For this reason many considered the prior, as head of the convent, to be culpably negligent. Later, when the time came to elect an abbot, our brother monks reminded one another of this. Our cellarer received all guests at the convent's expense, no matter what their circumstances. William the sacrist, in his office, acted with characteristic generosity, spending freely and giving away not only what should be given, but also what should not, 'blinding the eyes of all with gifts' [Deut. 16:19].

Samson the subsacrist, who was in charge of the workmen, left nothing broken, cracked, split, or unrepaired so far as he could, and thus won the esteem of the convent, and especially of the cloister monks. At this time he directed the building of our choir-screen and also arranged its narrative paintings and elegiac verses.* He had a great supply of stone and sand hauled up for the construction of the great tower of the church. When he was questioned as to the source of the money for all this, he replied that some of the townspeople had secretly given him cash to construct and complete the tower. But some of our brethren claimed that he and our monk Warin, who was warden of the shrine, had made a plot to withdraw a certain amount secretly from the offerings at the shrine to meet the essential expenses of the church, particularly those of the tower-building programme. It was said that they were persuaded to do this because they were aware that the offerings were being used for irregular purposes by others who—to be frank—were embezzling the funds. To avoid being suspected of theft, the two men made an offertory box, which was rounded, with a hole in the middle of the top, and was fastened with an iron bar, and this they got put up in the crossing of the great church, next to the door out of the choir so that passers-by would put into it their gifts for building the tower.

But William the sacrist was suspicious of his colleague Samson, and had the support of many others, both Christians and Jews. I should explain that the sacrist was referred to as the father and patron of the Jews, for they enjoyed his protection. They had free entrance and exit, and went everywhere throughout the monastery, wandering by the altars and round the shrine while Mass was being celebrated. Their money was deposited in our treasury, in the sacrist's custody. Even more incongruous, during the troubles [of 1173–4], their wives and children were sheltered in our pittancery.

These enemies and opponents of Samson worked out a plan to attack him. They approached Robert of Cockfield and his colleague, the custodians of the abbot's estates, and persuaded them to prohibit, on the king's behalf, the carrying out by anyone of any work or building while there was no abbot, and to order instead that cash from offerings should be collected and saved for repayment of any debt. In this way Samson was outwitted and 'his strength went from him' [Judg. 16:17, 19]: from that time he was unable to get his plans put into operation. However, although his adversaries were able to delay his work, they could not destroy it. When he had recovered his strength, and those two pillars were demolished [Judg. 16:29, 30]—I mean after the removal of the two custodians of the abbacy who had propped up the malice of others—the Lord gave Samson the power to fulfil his vow: in the course of time he built the tower, and thus achieved his dearest wish. It came about as if the divine voice said to him, 'Well done, good and faithful servant: thou hast been faithful over a few things, I will make thee ruler over many things' [Matt. 25:21].

During the vacancy, we often prayed to the Lord and to the holy martyr Edmund—as was our duty—to give us the right pastor for our church. Three times a week after coming out of chapter, we prostrated ourselves in choir to sing the seven penitential Psalms.* There were some who, if they had known the identity of the future abbot, would not have prayed so devoutly. On the question of electing an abbot, if the king would grant us a free election, many different views were expressed, some publicly, some privately. 'Every man had his own opinion' [Terence, *Phormio*, 454].

One man said of another, 'That brother is a good monk, a commendable person, who knows a great deal about the Rule and the customs of the church. Although not so complete a philosopher as some others, he might well make an abbot. Abbot Ording* was not educated, and yet he was a good abbot and governed this house wisely. In Aesop's

fables we read that it was better for the frogs to choose a
block of wood for their king, whom they could trust, than
a snake, who hissed venomously and after hissing devoured
his subjects.' Another replied, 'How is that possible? How
can an uneducated man preach a sermon, either in chapter
or to the people at festivals? How will a man who is ignorant
of scripture have the knowledge "to bind and to loose"
[Matt. 16:19]? The rule of souls is "the art of arts" [Gregory
the Great, *Pastoral Care*] and the science of sciences.
Heaven forbid that a speechless figurehead should be
promoted in St Edmund's church, where there are known
to be many educated and active men.'

In the same way, another man said of someone else,
'That brother is educated and eloquent, as well as careful
and strict in observing the Rule. He has shown great
devotion to the convent and has suffered a good deal for the
sake of the church's possessions. He deserves to become
abbot.' To which somebody replied, 'From good clerks, O
Lord, deliver us: that it may please Thee to preserve us
from all Norfolk tricksters, we ask Thee to hear us.'*

Similarly, someone said about another, 'That brother is a
good manager, as proved by the responsibility he has borne,
by his good service in various offices, and by the buildings
and repairs he has superintended. He certainly knows how
to work and take care of the domestic organization, and is
something of a scholar, although "too much learning will
not drive him mad" [Acts 26:24]. He is worthy of the office
of abbot.' To this someone answered, 'God does not want
as abbot a man who cannot read, or chant, or celebrate the
divine office. Nor does He want a dishonest or unjust man,
or an oppressor of the poor.'

Someone else said of another, 'That brother is a kind
man, approachable and lovable, a peacemaker and concilia-
tor, generous and open-handed, educated and eloquent, an
ideal man in appearance and style, well loved by many
inside and outside the monastery. If God wills it, the

appointment of such a man as abbot would bring great honour to the church.' Another replied, 'It would be no honour but an onus to have a man who is too fastidious over food and drink, and thinks it virtuous to sleep a lot; who knows how to spend much and get little; who snores while others are watchful; who always enjoys wealth, but is not concerned about the debts that are mounting daily, nor about how the expenses are to be met; who hates worry and hardship, not troubling so long as one day follows another; a man who favours and encourages flatterers and liars, and says one thing and does another. From such a leader may the Lord defend us.'

Then again, one man said of his colleague, 'That man is almost the wisest among us in both secular and ecclesiastical matters. He has good judgement and is very correct in his observance of the Rule, as well as being educated, eloquent, and of good personal standing. Such a leader would be appropriate for our church.' Someone else answered, 'True, if his reputation were certain and approved. Rightly or wrongly, there is some doubt about his character. Certainly, when he is a cloister monk he is a wise man, humble in chapter, devout in singing the Psalms, and strict in religious observance. Yet whenever he becomes an obedientiary he is inclined to be too impatient, scorning monks and choosing to be more intimate with laymen; and then, if he becomes angry, he will scarcely speak a word to any of the monks, not even in response to a question.'

I heard another brother rejected by certain others because he had a speech defect: it was said that he had dough or pig-food in his mouth when he had to speak. And I myself, then a young man, 'knew as a youth and spoke as a youth' [cf. 1 Cor. 13:11]: I said that I would not consent to anyone becoming abbot who did not know some dialectic and how to separate truth from falsehood. Someone who thought himself clever said, 'May Almighty God give us a foolish and inexperienced pastor, so that we shall have to assist him!' I heard that one man, hard-working, educated, and distinguished by his aristocratic birth, was excluded from consideration by some of our senior monks on the grounds that he was a junior. The young monks said that the senior monks were elderly and infirm, and incapable of governing the abbey. Thus many men said many things, and each one 'was fully persuaded in his own mind' [Rom. 14:5].

I once saw Samson the subsacrist sitting in the kind of little groups that used to form at blood-letting time,* when cloister monks would tell one another their private thoughts and discuss things together. I saw him sitting silently, smiling and noting what everyone else said, able to recall twenty years later [1201–2] some of the comments I have recorded above.

While he listened, I used to reply to those who were making the judgements, that if we must wait to elect an abbot until we found someone of quite blameless and spotless character, then we would never find such a person, because no one lives irreproachably, and 'nothing is entirely perfect' [Horace, *Odes*, II. xvi. 27]. Once, unable to restrain my high spirits, I rushed in to express my own opinion, believing that I spoke in confidence. I said that a certain person, who had previously been very fond of me and had been most generous to me, was not worthy to be abbot, and I went on to say that another person was worthy, naming someone whom I liked less. I was speaking according to my conscience, for the benefit of all rather than out of consideration for my own prospects of promotion; and I spoke the truth, as subsequent events showed. But imagine my horror when one 'of the sons of Belial' revealed my words to my friend and benefactor, and as a result, even to the present day I have been unable fully to regain his approval, either by appealing to him or by making gifts. What I said, I said [cf. John 19:22], and 'a word once uttered, speeds away beyond recall' [Horace, *Epistolae*, I. xviii. 71].

It remains for me to be careful in future, and if I live

long enough to see the abbacy vacant again, I shall watch what I say on the subject, and to whom and when I speak, so as to avoid offence either to God by telling lies or to man by speaking out of turn. However, if I survive till then, my judgement will be that we should elect someone who is not a very excellent monk, nor a very wise cleric, nor too ignorant or easy-going. If he is too clever, he may rely too much on himself and his own inclinations and disregard others, and if he is too unintellectual it would be scandalous. I understand the sayings: 'The safest path is in the middle' [Ovid, *Metamorphoses*, II. 137] and 'Blessed are those who keep to the middle ground'. Or perhaps it would be a more sensible policy to stay completely silent, telling myself, 'He that is able to receive it, let him receive it' [Matt. 19:12].

While the abbacy was vacant, Augustine, archbishop of Norway, stayed here in the abbot's lodgings, as the king had allowed him 10s. a day from the abbot's income.* He was very influential in obtaining our free election, testifying in our favour and speaking out publicly before the king from his own experience of us. It was at this time also [1181] that the saintly boy Robert was martyred and was buried in our church: many signs and wonders were performed among the people, as I have recorded elsewhere.*

The election of a new abbot 1182

A YEAR and three months after Abbot Hugh's death [i.e. late January or early February 1182], the king ordered in a letter that our prior and twelve members of the convent, who were to speak for us all, should appear in his presence on an appointed day to elect an abbot. The day after receiving the letter, we met together in chapter to discuss this very important matter. First the king's letter was read to the convent, and then we requested the prior, on peril of his soul, to carry out the task of nominating the twelve to accompany him, conscientiously choosing those whose way of life and conduct showed that they would not be deflected from doing right. Agreeing to this, the prior, with the guidance of the Holy Spirit, picked six from one side of the choir and six from the other,* and no objection being raised, we were all satisfied. From the right hand [south] side of the choir there were: Geoffrey of Fordham, Benedict, Master Denis, Master Samson the subsacrist, Hugh the third prior, and Master Hermer, then a young monk; and from the left [north]: William the sacrist, Andrew, Peter de Broc, Roger the cellarer, Master Ambrose, and Master Walter the physician.

But someone asked, 'What will happen if these thirteen men cannot agree in the king's court over the election of an abbot?' To which someone else replied that it would be a perpetual disgrace to us and our church. For this reason many wanted to have the election here before the others went off—a precaution designed to prevent dissension in the king's presence. But it seemed to us to be unwise and inappropriate to do this without royal permission, since it was not yet clear if the king would allow us a free election. Samson the subsacrist, inspired by the Holy Spirit, said, 'Let us follow the middle course so as to avoid danger at both extremes. Four confessors* and two of the most senior monks should be elected from the convent. They should be of good reputation, and after attending Mass and swearing on the gospels, they should choose from the convent the three men best qualified according to the Rule of St Benedict. They should write down the names of these, close the document with a wax seal, and give it to those of us who are going to the court. When we arrive in the king's presence and he agrees to our having a free election, then the seal should be broken and we should know the identity of the three to be nominated before the king. If the king refuses to allow us one of our own as abbot, the document, with the seal unbroken, should be brought back and

surrendered to the six sworn men, so that their secret may
be concealed forever on peril of their souls.' We all accepted
this plan, and four confessors were nominated—they were
Eustace, Gilbert of Elveden, Hugh the third prior, and
Antony—and two senior monks—Thurstan and Ruald.
Then we withdrew, chanting 'Ponder my words, O Lord'
[Ps. 5], and leaving the six to complete the arrangements as
agreed, with St Benedict's Rule to hand.

While the six were dealing with this, we discussed among
ourselves various suggestions about who should be chosen,
although we all thought it certain that Samson would be
one of the three nominees. We paid particular attention to
his hard work and to the way his life had been in danger on
his journey to Rome in the service of the church's possessions, and we recalled how he had been dragged off, put in
chains, and thrown into prison by Abbot Hugh for speaking
out in the interest of all—a man who could not be prevailed
upon to flatter, although he could be compelled to keep
silent.

After a delay, the convent was summoned to return to
the chapter-house, and the senior monks announced that
they had done as instructed. Then the prior enquired what
would happen if the king refused to choose any of the three
listed in the document. He was told that whoever the king
wished to support should be accepted, so long as he came
from our church. It was added also that if the thirteen
brothers noticed anything in the document that required
amendment, they were to amend it by God's will, with
general agreement. Samson the subsacrist, who sat at the
prior's feet, said that it would be best for the church 'if we
all take a solemn oath that whoever is elected will treat the
convent reasonably, not changing the chief obedientiaries
without the assent of the convent, nor putting an excessive
burden on the sacrist, nor making anyone a monk without
the convent's permission'. We agreed to this by a unanimous show of hands. In case the king might wish to appoint

an abbot from outside our monastery, there was a provision that the thirteen should not agree to an outsider except with the consent of the brothers who were remaining here.

Accordingly, those thirteen set out for the court the next day. Bringing up the rear was Samson, who as subsacrist was in charge of the expenses of the expedition and wore about his neck a letter-case containing the convent's documents. Without a bodyguard, and with his habit hitched up over his arms, he travelled to court following his companions at a distance, as if he were servant to the entire party.

On the journey, as the brothers talked together, Samson suggested that they should all swear that whoever became abbot would restore the churches of the convent's demesne to the hospitality fund. Everyone agreed to this except the prior, who said, 'We have sworn enough oaths: you could so weigh down the abbot that personally I would not care to have the job.' So they did not swear that oath, which was just as well, for even if sworn, it would not have been kept.

On the day the thirteen went away, one of our monks, William de Hastings,* told us as we sat in cloister, 'I am sure that we shall have one of our own as abbot'. When he was asked to explain, he said that he knew this from a dream. He had seen a prophet, dressed in white, standing at the monastery gate, and had enquired of him, in the Lord's name, whether we would have a monk of our own house as abbot. The prophet had replied, 'You shall have one of your own, but he will rage among you like a wolf.' This dream came partly true, since, as many used to say, the future abbot thought it more important to be feared than loved.

There was another brother sitting with us, whose name was Edmund. He maintained that Samson would be our next abbot and reported a vision that had appeared to him on the previous night. He told how in his sleep he had seen Roger the cellarer and Hugh the third prior standing before the altar, on either side of Samson, who was head and shoulders above them, and was wearing a long cloak that reached down to his ankles and was fastened at his shoulders: he stood like a fighter ready for combat. And the dreamer saw St Edmund rise up from the shrine and display his naked feet and legs like a sick man, and when someone approached as if to cover his feet the Saint said, 'Don't come any closer: look, there is the man who will clothe my feet', and pointed towards Samson. Samson's appearance as a fighter foretold that the future abbot would always be embattled, with contests at different times: with the archbishop of Canterbury over pleas of the crown, with the abbey's knights over the full payment of scutages, with the townsmen over encroachments in the market-place, and with the sokemen over the hundred courts.* Like a fighter he aimed in his struggles at overcoming his opponents, in order to recover the rights and liberties of his church. His covering of the holy martyr's feet points to his completion of the church towers that had been begun a hundred years earlier.* Dreams of this kind were being experienced by our brothers and accounts of them immediately circulated, first through the cloister and then through the courtyard, so that before evening the talk among the common people was: 'This one, and that one, and so-and-so have been chosen, and one of them is going to be abbot.'

Finally, on the second Sunday in Lent [21 February 1182], and after many troubles and delays, the prior and the twelve who had gone with him appeared before the king at Waltham [Hants],* a manor belonging to the bishop of Winchester. The king received them kindly, and stating that he wanted to proceed according to God's will and for the good of our church, he issued an order through intermediaries—Richard, bishop of Winchester and Geoffrey, the royal chancellor (later archbishop of York)*—that the brothers should select three candidates from the convent. The prior and brothers drew aside, as if to discuss the matter, and took out the document, and breaking the seal

found the following names written in this order: Samson
the subsacrist, Roger the cellarer, Hugh the third prior.
This ranking embarrassed the senior brothers, and everyone
was surprised that Hugh was both an elector and one of the
candidates. However, because they could not make a major
alteration, they agreed simply to change the order of the
names, putting Hugh first because he was third prior,
Roger the cellarer second, and Samson third—thus, as it
were, making 'the first last and the last first' [Matt. 19:30].

But the king, after asking whether they were born in his
dominions, and on whose estate, said that he did not know
them, and commanded another three to be nominated from
the convent in addition to the first three. When this was
agreed, William the sacrist said, 'The prior ought to be
nominated, as he is our head'. This was immediately
accepted. Then the prior said, 'William the sacrist is a good
man', and the same was said of Denis. Thus the matter was
settled. The king was surprised that they were nominated
there and then in his presence, and said, 'They have acted
very speedily. God is with them.'

Next, the king required that for the good of his kingdom,
they name three additional candidates from other monasteries. When they heard this, the brothers became apprehensive, suspecting a trick, but finally they formed a plan to
nominate three, with the proviso that no one could be
accepted without the approval of the members of the
convent who had remained at home. So they nominated
these three: Master Nicholas of Wallingford, now the abbot
of Malmesbury [1183-7]; Bertrand, prior of St Faith's
[Horsham, Norfolk], later abbot of Chertsey; and H[erbert,
prior] of St Neots, a monk of Bec,* a most religious man,
and also very prudent in both temporal and spiritual affairs.

When they had done this, the king thanked them and
directed that three names be eliminated from the nine:
whereupon the three outsiders' names were removed—that
is, the prior of St Faith's, later abbot of Chertsey, Nicholas

monk of St Albans, later abbot of Malmesbury, and the prior of St Neots. William the sacrist withdrew of his own accord, and after two of the remaining five had been eliminated on the king's orders, and later another one from the three, there were just two left, namely [Robert] the prior and Samson.

At this final stage the king's intermediaries, whom I mentioned earlier, were called in to attend the brothers' deliberations. Denis, speaking for everyone, began by commending both the prior and Samson, pointing out that both were educated, both were good, both led praiseworthy lives and had sound reputations. But throughout his speech the implication was that he favoured Samson: he spent more time on praising him, saying that his conduct was very proper, and that he was strict in correcting faults, capable of hard work, efficient in secular business, and of proven worth in positions of responsibility. The bishop of Winchester replied, 'We fully understand what you mean: from your comments we conclude that you consider your prior to be somewhat mild, and that you wish to have the man called Samson.' Denis answered, 'Both are good, but we should prefer the better one, if that is God's will.' To which the bishop said, 'Indeed, it is essential to pick the better of two good men. Tell me plainly, do you wish to have Samson?' The clear answer of the majority was 'We want Samson', and no one expressed a contrary opinion, although some deliberately kept silent, not wishing to offend either candidate. When Samson's name had been given to the king, he had a few words with his advisers, and then everyone was summoned to hear him say, 'You have presented Samson to me. I am not acquainted with him. If you had presented your prior I should have accepted him, as I already know him. But I will do as you wish. However, take care: by the very eyes of God, if you do wrong I shall personally take it out on you!' He then asked the prior if he was in full agreement with this, and the prior replied that he was, and that Samson was far worthier of the honour. Whereupon the elect prostrated himself and kissed the king's feet, then hurriedly got up and hastened to the altar,* chanting 'Have mercy upon me, O God' [Ps. 51] along with the brothers, his head up and his expression unchanged. When the king saw this, he said to bystanders, 'By God's eyes, this man considers himself worthy to take charge of the abbey.'

Abbot Samson installed—some innovations

THE arrival at the convent of the news of this election caused rejoicing among all, or nearly all, of the cloister monks, and a few, but only a few, of the obedientiaries. Many said, 'It is a good deed, well done.' But others said, 'No, on the contrary, we have all been misled.'

The elect, before he set out to return to us, was blessed by the bishop of Winchester,* who said, as he put the abbot's mitre on his head and the ring on his finger, 'These are the symbols of the high rank of the abbots of St Edmund's: long have I known this.' So the abbot, keeping three monks with him, sent the others home in advance, announcing that he would arrive on Palm Sunday [21 March 1182], and entrusting some of them with the arrangements for his feast.

As he was on his way back, a horde of new relatives hastened to him, wishing to be taken into his service, but he told them all that he was quite content with the prior's servants, and could not accept any others until he had consulted his convent. However, he did take on one knight who was eloquent and had knowledge of the law, not so much on account of his blood relationship, but because his experience in worldly affairs would be useful. In Samson's early days as abbot, this knight was his assistant in secular disputes, for Samson was new to the abbacy and ignorant of such matters. As he himself admitted, before he became abbot he had never been in a place where securities were given.*

It was with due ceremony, including a procession, that the lord abbot was received by his convent on Palm Sunday, as I shall now describe. He had spent the previous night at Kentford,* and since we had ample notice, after our chapter meeting we went out to meet him at the cemetery gate, with all solemnity, sounding the bells both inside the choir and outside. He arrived with a great throng of people pressed round him, but when he saw the convent he dismounted from his horse outside the gate and had his shoes removed. Then he was brought barefoot through the gate, with the prior and the sacrist conducting him on either side. As we led the abbot to the high altar, we chanted the responses— 'Blessed be the Lord God of Israel' from the office for Trinity Sunday, and then 'The martyr's still . . .' from the office for the Feast of St Edmund. After this the organ and bells were silent, the abbot prostrated himself, and the prior said over him the prayer 'Almighty and eternal God, have mercy upon this, etc.' Then the abbot made a gift to the church, kissed the shrine, and returned to the choir, where he was received by Samson the precentor, who led him by the hand to the abbot's stall at the west end. There, while the abbot remained standing, the precentor immediately began the 'Te Deum', and during the singing of this, the abbot was kissed by the prior and the whole convent in order.

When this was over, the abbot went into the chapter-house, followed by the convent and many other people. After an exchange of blessings, he first thanked the convent for having elected him to be their lord and pastor, not for any merit of his own, for he was, he said, the least important of them all, but because it was God's will. In a few words he requested their prayers, and then turned to speak to the clerks and knights. He asked them if they would advise him on the concerns of his office. To this Wimer the sheriff replied, on behalf of the rest, 'As you are the dear lord whom God has chosen for His own sake and for the sake of the holy martyr Edmund, we shall surely support you with advice and assistance in every way.' Then the king's charters relating to the appointment of the abbot were brought out and read in the hearing of all. After the abbot had prayed that God would take care of him according to His grace, and everyone had answered 'Amen', the convent went to the first Mass. After this the abbot, still barefoot, proceeded to his lodgings for a celebration feast, a very joyful occasion, with more than 1,000 dining together.*

When all this happened, I was chaplain to [Robert] the prior, and within four months I became chaplain to the abbot. There was much that I observed and committed to memory. On the day following his feast, the abbot called together the prior and a few others, as if to ask their advice: in fact, 'he himself knew what he would do' [John 6:6]. He said that a new seal should be made showing the mitre,* although his predecessors had not had such a seal. Until then Samson had used the seal of our prior, noting at the end of each letter that as he did not have his own seal he was using the prior's for the time being. Later he made the arrangements for his household, appointing several assistants to various offices, and stated that he planned to stable twenty-six horses in his courtyard. He asserted that 'a child has first to crawl before he can stand and walk steadily'. He instructed his staff that they were to ensure above all that in his early days as abbot he could not be accused of meanness with food and drink, and that they were to give careful attention to the hospitality of his house.

In arranging and settling these matters, as all others, he put complete trust in God's help and in his own common sense, considering it degrading to rely on another's advice, as if his own opinion alone were enough. This surprised the monks and angered the knights, who condemned his arrogance and in some measure discredited him at the king's court, saying that he would not bother himself with the views of his free tenants. He excluded from his private circle of counsellors all the greater tenants of the abbey, both lay and literate,* without whose advice and assistance it was thought that the abbey could not be properly governed. For this reason Ranulph de Glanville, the justiciar of England, was at first suspicious of Samson and less well disposed towards him than he should have been, until the evidence convinced him beyond doubt that the abbot was conducting both the internal and the external affairs of the abbey skilfully and wisely.

In answer to a general summons, all the barons, knights, and free tenants came to do homage* on the fourth day of Easter [31 March 1182]. And Thomas de Hastings had the effrontery to come with a large number of knights, bringing his nephew Henry, who had not yet been knighted, for whom he claimed the office of steward* and its customary rights according to the nephew's charter. The abbot told him straight out, 'I do not and will not deny Henry his rights. If he were capable of performing the duties himself, then I would allow him maintenance in my household with ten men and eight horses, as stated in his charter. If you present me with someone to act as steward on his behalf, who has the necessary knowledge to perform the office, then I will take him on the same conditions as applied on the day of my predecessor's death, that is with four horses and so forth. If you will not agree, I shall take the case to the king or the chief justice.' After this speech by the abbot, the affair was delayed for a while. Later, a naïve and inexperienced man, named Gilbert [de Hastings], was presented to him as steward. Before he accepted him, the abbot said to his closest associates, 'If through this steward's ignorance there is any failure in upholding the king's justice, he, and not I, will be answerable to the king, because he claims the stewardship by hereditary right. Therefore for the time being I would rather take him than be cheated by a cleverer man. With God's help I shall be my own steward.'

When the abbot had taken the homages, he requested an aid* from his knights, and they promised £1 each. But they then went into urgent consultation together and subtracted £12 for twelve knights,* saying that those twelve were bound to assist the other forty, not only in performing the duty of castle-guard and in rendering scutages, but also in paying the abbot's aid. This made the abbot very angry when he heard it, and he told his close advisers that if he lived he would get even with them by paying them injury for injury.

Then the abbot had enquiries made in every manor that belonged to the abbacy about the annual rents paid by the free tenants, and the names of the unfree tenants, with their holdings and services. Everything was to be put down in writing. Furthermore, he repaired the manor-houses and domestic buildings that were so old and derelict that birds of prey* and crows flew in and out of them. He built new chapels and added domestic apartments in many manors where previously there had been no buildings other than barns. He created several parks which he stocked with game, and he retained a huntsman with hounds. If any important guest was being entertained, the abbot would sit with his monks in a woodland clearing to watch the hounds giving chase, but I never saw him eat the meat of hunted animals. In his great concern to do everything to the advantage of the abbacy, he had many pieces of land taken in from the wild and ploughed up for cultivation, but I wish that he had taken a similar care over the manors belonging to the convent. He did, however, take our manors of Bradfield [Bradfield Combust] and Rougham into his own management for a time, giving us £40 in compensation for lost rent, though he restored them later, after he heard that there were complaints in the convent about his keeping our manors in his own control.

To run these and all the manors, he appointed new custodians, both monks and laymen, who were more astute than the previous ones, and would look after us and our estates more wisely. The eight hundreds in his own management and the [half] hundred of Cosford, which he recovered on the death of Robert of Cockfield [1190], he put into the hands of officials who belonged to his own household. He reserved for himself the more important decisions, delegating the less important to others, and twisting everything to his own profit.

On his order a complete survey was made, in each hundred, of letes, suits, hidages, foddercorn,* renders of hens, and other customs, rents, and payments, which had always been largely concealed by the tenants. Everything was written down, so that within four years of his election [i.e. 1186], no one could cheat him of a penny of the abbacy rents, and this despite the fact that no documents relating to the administration of the abbey had been handed on to him from his predecessors (except one short list giving the names of St Edmund's knights, the names of the manors, and the rents due from the farms). This was the book he called his 'Kalendar'.* It also contained details of every debt he had paid off. He looked in this book nearly every day, as though it were a mirror reflecting his own integrity.

On the first day that he held a chapter meeting, he confirmed to us, using his new seal, the £3 from Southery [Norf.] which his predecessors had wrongly accepted from Edmund, nicknamed 'the golden monk', for a life-lease on the village. And he issued an order that in future no one was to pawn any ornaments of the church without the convent's agreement, which had been a common practice, nor was any charter to be sealed with the convent's seal, except in the convent's presence at a chapter meeting. He appointed Hugh as subsacrist, directing that William the sacrist was to have nothing whatever to do with the duties of the office, neither with receipts nor with expenses, except with Hugh's permission.

Following this, though not on the same day, he transferred the former wardens of the offerings-fund to other departments. And in the end he deposed William himself. This caused William's friends to exclaim, 'See the abbot now! There's the wolf of the dream! Look how he rages!' and some wanted to plot against the abbot. When he was told of this, he resolved neither to remain completely silent nor to upset the convent, so when he came into chapter the next day he produced a bag full of cancelled charters, still bearing their seals, some in his predecessor's name, some in the prior's, some the sacrist's, some the chamberlain's, and some in the names of other officials. The total of the capital involved was £3,052 and 1 mark, without the accumulated interest, whose real magnitude could never be known. He had come to terms over all these debts within a year of his election, and he had paid them all off inside twelve years. 'Take a look at the wise policies of your sacrist William!' he said. 'Just see how many charters have been sealed by him without the convent's consent, pledging silk copes, dalmatics, silver thuribles, and volumes bound in gold,* all of which I have repurchased and restored to you.' He went on to give further justification of his deposition of William, although he did not reveal the principal reason as he did not wish to 'cause him to stumble' [Mal. 2:8]. Then he appointed Samson the precentor to be sacrist in William's place, and thus everything was resolved peacefully, since Samson was superior in every way and was acceptable to us all. The abbot even ordered the sacrist's house in the cemetery to be completely demolished, as if it were not fit to stand upon the earth, on account of the frequent drinking sessions and other unmentionable activities of which he had been made painfully aware as subsacrist. Within a year he had it all razed to the ground: where a fine building had stood we saw beans pushing up their stems, and where wine barrels had been stored there grew a bed of nettles.

When Easter week was over [5 April 1182], the abbot visited each of his own manors and ours, confirming the farm tenants in each, and demanding from everyone an aid and recognition,* according to the custom of the realm. His skill in secular affairs increased daily as he directed his attention to familiarizing himself with the conduct of the monastery's business with the outside world.

One night, when he was staying at Warkton [Northants], he heard a voice speaking to him in his sleep, 'Samson, get up quickly', and then, 'Get up, you are too slow.' Astonished, he got up and looked around, and saw a light in the lavatory. It was a candle that was just about to fall on to some straw, carelessly left there by the monk Reiner. After he had snuffed out the candle, he went round the house and found the only door fastened in such a way that it could not be opened without a key and the windows tightly closed, so that if the fire had flared up, that would have been the end of him and all the people sleeping in that room, because there was no exit or escape route.

Wherever the abbot travelled at that time, both Jews and Christians rushed to meet him, demanding payment of debts, and they so worried and distressed him that he lost sleep and grew pale and thin. He said, 'My mind will never be at rest until I know that I am out of debt.'

When Michaelmas [29 September 1182] arrived he took all his manors into his own management, with their meagre farm equipment and livestock. He waived £19 of the previous year's rent due from Walter of Hatfield, in return for the surrender of four manors which had been confirmed to Walter by Abbot Hugh—Hargrave, Saxham, Chevington, and Stapleford [Stapleford Abbotts, Essex]. But he postponed recovering Harlow [Essex] for the following reason. On one occasion it happened that we were passing through a forest on our return from London, when, in the abbot's hearing, I asked a little old lady whom we met what forest this was, and to what village it belonged, and who was the landlord or custodian? She replied that the forest belonged to the abbot of St Edmund's, that the village was Harlow, and that a man called Arnold was the custodian. When I enquired how Arnold behaved towards the village people, she answered that he had been a living devil, an enemy of God and an oppressor of the peasantry, 'but now he fears the new abbot of St Edmund's, whom he considers to be wise and careful, and so he treats the tenantry more gently'. On hearing this the abbot was delighted, and decided not to take over the manor himself for a while.

At that time the unexpected news arrived of the death of Herlewin of Runcton's wife, who held that village [North Runcton, Norf.] by charter, on a lease for her lifetime. The abbot said, 'Yesterday I would have given 60 marks to get that manor; now the Lord has delivered it to me for nothing.' He set out immediately to repossess the village, and arrived the following day at Tilney [Tilney cum Islington, Norf.], which was part of the same manor. There a knight came and offered him 30 marks to be allowed to hold that carucate* of land [in Tilney], with its appurtenances, for its old rent of £4. The abbot refused, and that year he made £25 from the land and the next year £20.

These and similar events caused him to keep everything under his own direction: as one may read elsewhere, 'Caesar was all in all' [Lucan, *Pharsalia*, III. 108]. He did not act slowly, but began straight away to build barns and cowsheds. He was anxious above all to farm the land profitably, and he freely acknowledged that in taking care of the woodlands he kept a jealous eye on any grants or reductions. He confirmed only one manor by charter: that was Thorpe, held by an Englishman, a free man, though tied to the soil, of whose loyalty he was confident, because he was a good farmer and could not speak French.

Samson's character

LESS than seven months after his election [so before 28 September 1182], he was surprised to receive from the pope a mandate appointing him a judge delegate to hear certain cases.* Although he was well versed in the liberal arts* and the scriptures, a cultured man who had been at university,* and had been a well-known and highly regarded schoolmaster in his own region, he was untutored and inexperienced in canon law. Therefore he invited two clerks with legal training to be his companions, and used their advice in ecclesiastical matters. He gave his attention to the *Decretum* and to decretal letters* when he had time, and before long, partly by the study of books and partly by hearing cases, he came to be considered a discerning judge who followed the law and its procedure closely. For this reason someone was heard to say, 'Curses on the court of that abbot, where neither gold nor silver is of any use to me in defeating my adversary!'

As time went on, and relying on his innate intelligence, he became quite experienced in secular cases, and his precise mind was admired by everyone. The under-sheriff, Osbert son of Hervey, said of him, 'This abbot is a natural investigator, and if he continues as he has started, he will blind every one of us with his science.' Having gained a favourable reputation in cases of this kind, he was made an itinerant justice,* but he did not allow himself to stray from the correct path.

But 'envy aims at the highest' [Ovid, *Rem. Amor.*, 369]. It was reported that he refused justice to plaintiffs unless influenced by gifts or promises of money, because when his tenants took their cases to him in St Edmund's court he refused to give hasty judgements or 'believe every spirit' [1 John 4:1], but acted in accordance with judicial process, knowing that the merits of cases emerge from the evidence of the parties. And because he had a sharp and perceptive

eye, and a stern expression that rarely softened, he was said
to be more inclined to severity than kindness. And in
dealing with fines for any offence, he was said to exalt
judgement above mercy [cf. Jas. 2:13] because, as it seemed
to many, when it came to taking money, only rarely did he
accept less than the maximum.

As his wisdom increased, so also did his carefulness in
the management and improvement of property and in
making proper arrangements for expenses. But here, too,
many carping critics claimed that he took what he wanted
from the sacrist's department, saving his own money and
keeping back his corn until it could command the maximum
price, and that unlike his predecessors he spent time on his
manors, burdening the cellarer with guests whose entertainment was really the abbot's responsibility. It was said that
by these means he would be able to appear wise, prosper-
ous, and far-sighted at the end of the year, while the
convent and obedientiaries would seem uninformed and
feckless.

I used to rebut these criticisms by saying that if he took
anything out of the sacrist's fund he spent it to the
advantage of the church, and this not even his worst enemy
could deny. In fact, much more important and numerous
benefits came from the use of the sacristy offerings in the
fifteen years after his election than in all the previous forty
years. To the objection that the abbot tended to stay at his
manors, I would reply by explaining, 'the abbot is more
cheerful and lively away from home'. It was certainly true
that at home, either because of the crowds of plaintiffs who
flocked to him or because of rumour-mongers, he often
wore such a stern expression that he lost much of the
goodwill and gratitude of his guests, even though they were
pleased with the food and drink he provided.

Having this in mind, when I had an opportunity and was
close to him, I said privately, 'There are two things about
you that perplex me very much.' When he asked what the

two things were, I said, 'Firstly, even in your present position you still cherish the academic notion* that a false premiss leads nowhere, and similar nonsensical ideas.' He replied to this as he saw fit. Then I went on, 'Secondly, there is no doubt that at home you put on a less agreeable face than when away, even with the brothers, who love you now as they did when they elected you to be their abbot. They say that when you associate with them—which you do only occasionally—you do not share in their conviviality.' When he heard this his face changed and he hung his head as he replied, 'You are a fool and you speak foolishly. You should know what Solomon says, "Thou hast many daughters. Show not thy face cheerful towards them" [Ecclus. 7:26].' That certainly silenced me, and in future I watched what I said. But on another occasion I commented, 'Father, last night after Matins* I heard you unusually wakeful and sighing deeply.' He answered, 'That is no cause for surprise. You share in my wealth—in food and drink and travel and so on—but you scarcely give a thought to the things that worry me—the administration of the abbey and of my household, and the many difficult matters that I encounter in my pastoral role. These are the things that cause me misery and heartache.' In reply I raised my hands to the heavens: 'Almighty and merciful Lord, grant that I may be spared such anxieties.'

I heard the abbot say that if he could have returned to the circumstances he had enjoyed before he became a monk, with 5 or 6 marks a year to keep himself at the university, he would never have become a monk or abbot. On another occasion he swore that if he could have foreseen the nature and scope of the abbot's duties, rather than be abbot and lord, he would have been master of the aumbry and librarian,* which was the office he had always wanted above all others. Who could believe that? I scarcely could, nor would I have done, if I had not lived with him day and night for six years [1182–8], and become completely familiar with the worthiness of his life and his exemplary wisdom.

He once told the story of how, when he was a boy of 9, he dreamt that he was standing in front of the cemetery gate of St Edmund's, when the devil, with outstretched arms, tried to seize him, but St Edmund was near and rescued him, taking him in his arms. As he cried out in his dream, 'Help me, St Edmund!' (a name he had never heard before), he woke up. His mother was astounded, as much by what he shouted as by the vehemence of his cry, and when he told her his dream she took him to pray at St Edmund's shrine. As they arrived at the cemetery gate he exclaimed, 'Mother, this is the place! Look, that is the gate I saw in my dream when the devil tried to take me.' He used to say that he knew the place even before he saw it with his own eyes. The abbot himself interpreted the dream: the devil represented worldly pleasure which would have tempted him, but St Edmund embraced him, wishing him to become a monk of his church.

One day, when he was told that some members of the convent were grumbling about something he had done, he said to me as I sat beside him, 'God, Oh God! I would do better to remember the dream that was narrated about me before I was made abbot, that I would rage as a wolf. As a matter of fact, what I fear most in all the world is that my convent will do something that will make me rage. But when they say or do something contrary to my wishes, I recall that dream, and though I rage inwardly, secretly growling and grinding my teeth, I force myself not to rage in what I say or do, and "my suppressed grief chokes me and seethes within me" [Ovid, *Tristia*, v. i. 63].' Although he was naturally quick-tempered and easily provoked, yet for the sake of his high position he usually controlled his anger, even if it was with a considerable effort. Indeed, he sometimes boasted of this, saying, 'I saw this and that, and I heard such and such, and nevertheless I kept my patience'.

Once when he was sitting in chapter, the abbot made a remark that might be interpreted as seeking popularity with the convent. 'I do not want anyone coming to me with an accusation against another that he is not prepared to make openly. If anyone disregards this, I shall make the accuser's name public. Also I should like every cloister monk to feel free to come to me whenever he wishes, to have a talk with me about his needs.' He said this because in Abbot Hugh's time the most powerful among us, wishing to control everything that was done in the monastery, forbade any cloister monk to talk with the abbot without first revealing to the abbot's chaplain exactly what he wished to say.

One day he made an order in chapter that anyone who possessed a seal of his own should surrender it to him. When this was done, the total was found to be thirty-three seals. The reason for the order became clear when he prohibited any official from taking on any debt of more than £1—which had been a common practice—without the assent of the prior and convent. But he returned their seals to the prior and to the sacrist, while keeping all the others. On another day he ordered all keys to chests, cupboards, and hanapers* to be handed in to him, forbidding anyone in future to have a chest or anything locked up without permission, or to possess any item at any time that was not allowed in the Rule. He did, however, grant general permission that we could each have cash up to 2s. to spend on poor relations or in other pious works, provided we had been given it as a charitable donation.

Another time, the abbot announced that he would retain our customary practice in the entertainment of guests:* that is, when the abbot is at home he shall himself receive all guests, whatever their circumstances, except religious and secular clergy, and their followers, who have tended to

present themselves at the courtyard gate and claim hospitality as hangers-on. If the abbot is not at home, all guests,
whatever their circumstances, but with a maximum of
thirteen horses, are to be received by the cellarer. But if a
layman or clergyman shall come with more than thirteen
horses, he shall be received by the abbot's servants, either
inside or outside the courtyard, at the abbot's expense. The
entertainment of all religious, including bishops if they
happen to be monks, belongs to the cellarer, and is charged
to the convent, unless the abbot chooses to honour any of
them by receiving them in his own hall at his own expense.

Abbot Samson was of medium height and almost completely bald. His face was neither round nor long, and he
had a prominent nose and thick lips. His eyes were crystal
clear, with a penetrating gaze, and he had extremely sharp
hearing. His eyebrows were bushy and were frequently
trimmed. As soon as he caught a slight cold he became
hoarse. On the day of his election [28 February 1182] he
was 47 years of age, and had been a monk for seventeen
years. There were then only a few grey hairs in his red
beard and very few indeed in his hair, which was black and
wavy, but within fourteen years of his election he had
turned as white as snow. He was a very serious-minded
man and was never idle. His health was excellent, and he
liked to travel on horseback or on foot, until he was
prevented by old age.

When he heard the news of the loss of the Holy Cross
and the fall of Jerusalem [1187],* he began to wear breeches
of hair cloth and a hairshirt instead of one made of mixed
wool and linen. He also began to abstain from meat and
dishes containing meat. He asked, however, for helpings of
meat to be brought to him at table, so as to increase the
food given away to the poor. He enjoyed sweetened milk,
honey, and similar sweet things more than any other food.
Because goodness is attracted to its own likeness and rejects
its opposite, he detested lies, drunkenness, and verbosity.

He disapproved of people complaining about food and drink, particularly if the grumblers were monks, and he himself, continuing to conduct his life as he had in his earlier days as a cloister monk, practised the virtuous habit of never attempting to change any dish of food that was set before him. When I was a novice, I wanted to test the truth of this, so when I happened to be serving in the refectory, I thought to myself that I would give him some food that would be distasteful to anybody else, on a very black and broken plate. When he saw it, he acted as if he had not noticed. After a little while I was ashamed of what I had done, so I quickly snatched up the plate and brought him instead some better food on a better plate. But he was angry and upset, and made a fuss about accepting the substitute.

He was a good speaker, in both French and Latin, concentrating more on plain speaking than on flowery language. He could read books written in English most elegantly, and he used to preach to the people in English, but in the Norfolk dialect, for that was where he was born and brought up.* He gave orders for a pulpit to be erected, both to enhance the beauty of the church and also to allow the congregation to hear the sermons clearly. The abbot appeared to prefer the active to the contemplative life, in that he praised good obedientiaries more highly than good cloister monks, and rarely commended anyone solely for his knowledge of literature unless he also knew about secular matters. When he chanced to hear of any church leader resigning his pastoral work to become a hermit, he would not utter one word of commendation.

He was unwilling to lavish praise on good-natured men, commenting, 'He who strives to please all is bound to please none.' Thus, in his first year of office he regarded all flatterers, especially monks, with something approaching hatred, but as time went by he seemed to listen to them more willingly and treat them more as friends. So it happened that when one of our brothers, who was a master of the art, knelt down before him, and while pretending to give some advice, filled his ears with unctuous compliments, I smiled to myself as I stood watching from a distance. But when the monk had gone, the abbot called me over and asked me why I had smiled. I replied that the world was full of flatterers. The abbot answered, 'My son, I have known flatterers for many years, and therefore I cannot avoid hearing them. I am forced into many shams and pretences to keep the convent peaceful. I shall listen to what they say, but if I can help it they will not deceive me as they deceived my predecessor. He foolishly relied on their advice, so that long before he died he had nothing for himself or his household to eat, except what was bought on credit. There was nothing to be distributed to the poor on the day of his funeral, except 50s. received from Richard the lessee of Palgrave because he happened to have taken over the lease of Palgrave on that very day; but even this money had to be given up to the king's bailiffs later, when they demanded the whole rent on the king's behalf.'* I took comfort from these words.

The abbot was anxious that his household should be well ordered and no larger than necessary. He took care that the weekly allowance, which under his predecessor had not met five days' outgoings, should last him eight, nine, or ten days, if he was staying on his manors and there was no great influx of guests. Every week, instead of being represented by a deputy, he personally attended the audit of his household expenses, which had never been his predecessor's practice. In his first seven years, dinner in his household consisted of four courses, but after that only three, excluding special dishes for guests and game from his parks or fish from his fish-ponds. If at any time, responding to the request of some important person or friend, he employed any page-boys or harpists or anyone of that kind in his household, he wisely got rid of such unnecessary

extras as soon as an opportunity arose of travelling abroad
or of going on a long journey.

Those monks who had been the abbot's most cherished
friends and companions before his election were rarely
appointed as obedientiaries on the strength of their old
association, unless they were also right for the job. This
caused some of those who had favoured his election as
abbot to say that he showed less affection towards them
than was appropriate, and that he was fonder of those who
had slandered him, both publicly and privately, and in the
hearing of many people had even branded him as an
irascible, unsociable, arrogant Norfolk trickster. But as he
indulged in no injudicious displays of affection or favour
towards his old friends after his election, so by the same
token he did not repay the many others with any sign of
resentment or enmity: he rendered good for evil, and did
good to those who persecuted him [cf. Rom. 12:17, 21;
Matt. 5:44]. He also had a characteristic (unique in my
experience) of never, or very seldom, showing in his face
any sign of the affection he felt for a good many people.
This is quite contrary to the proverb, 'The heart's letter is
written in the eye.' Another remarkable feature of his
character was that he knowingly sustained the damage and
loss his servants caused to his possessions, and admitted
that he did so: but I think it was because he would wait for
the right time to have the matter rectified, or else seek to
avoid further loss by practising this deception.

Since his relatives were no closer to him than first
cousin—or so he made out—he gave them only moderate
attention, and did not show excessive favour as some do. I
heard him say that he was related to some of the nobility,
but he would never openly acknowledge them as members
of his family, because he said that if they knew of the
relationship they would be more of a burden to him than
an asset. He preferred to regard as kindred those who had
treated him as a kinsman when he had been just a poor

cloister monk. Some of these—but only the ones he considered useful and properly qualified—he appointed to various posts in his household and as custodians of his manors. Those who proved to be unreliable, on the other hand, were turned out once and for all.

He treated as a dear and close relative one man of middling status, who had loyally preserved his inheritance and served him devotedly when he was young. To this man's son, who was a clergyman, he gave the first parish church that became vacant after he took over the abbacy, and he advanced the careers of all the other sons.

A chaplain, who by selling holy water had supported him when he was a poor student at Paris university, he called to him, and, in a reversal of roles, rewarded with a church appointment that would support him.

To the servant of Abbot Hugh who had put Samson in leg-irons, acting on his master's orders when Samson was in prison, he now granted free food and clothing for the rest of his life.

When the son of Elias came to do homage for the land which had been held by his father, Abbot Hugh's butler,* Samson said to him in the full feudal court, 'I have delayed taking your homage for seven years, because the land your father received from Abbot Hugh was taken out of the manor of Elmswell, to its loss: but now I have decided to do so, remembering with gratitude your father's action when I was in chains and he sent me some of his master's wine, with the message that I should take comfort in God.'

To Master Walter, son of Master William of Diss, who asked him to be so kind as to give him the vicarage of Chevington, he replied, 'Your father was my schoolmaster, who, when I was a poor clerk, charitably allowed me free entry and instruction at his school: so now, for the love of God, I grant what you ask.'

When two knights of Risby, one called William and the other Norman, were found guilty of offences that carried fines,* he addressed them in his court as follows: 'In my days as a cloister monk, on one occasion I was returning home from Durham, where I had been sent on our church's business, when I arrived at Risby at nightfall. I asked Norman if he would give me a bed for the night, but he utterly refused. When I went on to William's house with the same request, he received me courteously. Therefore I shall exact the full £1 fine from Norman, but William, on the other hand, I thank, and freely pardon his fine of £1.'

A young girl, who begged food from door to door, complained to the abbot that one of the sons of Richard, son of Drogo, had raped her. The abbot arranged a settlement whereby she was awarded one mark, and Richard paid the abbot 4 marks for making the settlement. Then the abbot ordered the total sum, 5 marks, to be given at once to a merchant, on condition that he marry the little beggar girl.

In St Edmund's town the abbot bought some stone-built houses, which he gave to the schoolmaster for use as lodgings for poor clerks. This freed them for ever from having to rent accommodation, which had previously cost each of them, rich and poor, a penny or halfpenny twice a year.

The Jews expelled—the purchase of Mildenhall 1190

THE abbot's repurchase of the manor of Mildenhall for as little as 1,100 marks of silver, the expulsion of the Jews from St Edmund's town, and the foundation of the new hospital at Babwell are all signs of his great goodness.

The abbot asked the king [in 1190] for written permission to expel the Jews from St Edmund's town, on the grounds that everything in the town and within the *banleuca* belonged by right to St Edmund: therefore, either the Jews should be St Edmund's men or they should be banished from the town. Accordingly, he was given permission to turn them out, but they were to retain their movable possessions and also the value of their houses and lands. When they had been escorted out and taken to various other towns by an armed troop, the abbot directed that in future all those who received back Jews or gave them lodging in St Edmund's town, were to be excommunicated in every church and at every altar.* Later, however, the king's justices ruled that if Jews came to the abbot's great court of pleas to claim debts from their debtors, they could for this purpose be given two days' and two nights' lodging in the town, and on the third day they should leave in freedom.

The abbot offered 500 marks to King Richard [in 1190] for the manor of Mildenhall, saying that it was worth £70 a year and was entered at that value in the Great Roll of Winchester.* He was hopeful of success, but at that point the matter was adjourned to the next day. Meanwhile someone went to the king and told him that the manor was worth a good £100 annually. So the next day, when the abbot followed up his petition, the king said, 'You ask in vain, Father abbot: either you will give me 1,000 marks or you will not have the manor.' Now whenever King Richard took 1,000 marks, Queen Eleanor customarily received 100 marks,* so on this occasion she accepted from us a great chalice of gold, worth 100 marks, which she then gave back to us for the soul of her husband, King Henry [II], who had originally given it to St Edmund. Another time, when the treasure of our church was sent to London for King Richard's ransom [1193],* the Queen redeemed the chalice for 100 marks and restored it to us in exchange for a charter solemnly promising that we would never again allow the chalice out of the church's possession for any reason whatsoever.

The huge sum of 1,000 marks was scraped together with

great difficulty, and when the transaction was complete the abbot announced in chapter that a proportion of the manor's ample profits belonged to him. The convent agreed that this was just: 'Thy will be done' [Matt. 6:10]. But the abbot said that although he would be within his rights in claiming half, as he had struggled to make his contribution of more than 400 marks to the purchase price, nevertheless he would be satisfied with part of another manor, called Icklingham. This was readily conceded by the convent. At this the abbot said, 'I am taking over this land, not to retain it in my own possession, nor to give it to members of my family, but to use for the good of our souls—both mine and yours—by donating it to the new hospital at Babwell,* so that it may provide food for the poor and accommodation for travellers.' This was done as he said, and was afterwards confirmed by royal charter.

Abbot Samson performed these and similar deeds, worthy of eternal record and renown, but he himself said that he would have achieved nothing in his lifetime unless he could accomplish the dedication of our church.* When this had been done, he declared, he would be ready to die. He said he was prepared to spend 2,000 silver marks on the dedication ceremony, provided it was attended by the king in person and was conducted with all solemnity.

Samson's journey to Rome c.1159–60

WHEN the abbot was informed that the church of Woolpit had become vacant on the election of Walter of Coutances to the bishopric of Lincoln [8 May 1183],* he summoned the prior and the greater part of the convent and told them the following story. 'You are well aware of the great trouble I have had over the church of Woolpit. To secure your control over it I went to Rome on your behalf [c.1159–60] during the schism between Pope Alexander and Octavian.* I travelled through Italy at a time when all clergymen carrying letters from Pope Alexander were arrested: some were imprisoned, some were hanged, and some had their noses and lips disfigured, and were then sent back to the pope, to humiliate and distress him. But I pretended to be a Scotsman, wearing Scottish dress and behaving like a Scot. To drive off those who jeered at me, I brandished my stick as if it were a type of spear known as a "gaveloc",* and used threatening language as Scotsmen do. When I was stopped and asked who I was, the only answer I would give was, "Ride, ride Rome, turn Canterbury."* I did this to conceal my identity and my plan, so that disguised as a Scot I could reach Rome more safely.

'After I had obtained the letter I sought from the pope, the road back from Rome led me past a castle. Then a dreadful thing happened: the retainers from this fortress surrounded me and took me captive, with the words, "This lonely wanderer, making himself out to be a Scot, is either a spy or the bearer of letters from Alexander, the false pope." They set about searching my tattered clothing, my boots and breeches, and even the old slippers that I carried over my shoulders in the Scottish manner, but as they did so I put my hand under my little drinking cup and into the leather bag containing the pope's letter, and by the will of God and of St Edmund, I took out the document and the cup together in such a way that when I stretched out my arm I held the letter beneath the cup.* They saw the cup but did not notice the letter, and that was how, in the Lord's name, I was able to escape from them. They stole all the money I had, so that I was penniless and forced to beg from door to door all the way back to England.

'But when I heard that the church had been given to Geoffrey Ridel* I was saddened and disheartened that all my labour had been in vain. On my return home I took refuge under St Edmund's shrine, afraid that the abbot would arrest and imprison me, although I had certainly not deserved punishment.* None of the monks ventured to speak to me, and there was no layman who dared bring me food, except surreptitiously. Finally, when he had taken advice, the abbot exiled me to Acre [Castle Acre, Norf.], where I stayed for a long while.

'I experienced these and numerous other misfortunes on account of the church of Woolpit, but, praise God, who "works all things together for good" [Rom. 8:28], that very same church, for which I endured so much suffering, has come into my own possession, and now that it is vacant I have the power to grant it as I choose. I restore to you, the convent, the annual payment of 10 marks which used to be made from that church, and which you lost more than sixty years ago [1123 or earlier]. I would gladly give you the whole income of the church if I could, but I know that the bishop of Norwich [John of Oxford, 1175–1200] would oppose this, or, if he did allow it, would use the occasion to claim subjection and obedience from you, which would be unacceptable and inappropriate. Therefore, we must act according to the letter of the law. Let us appoint a clergyman as vicar, who will pay "spirituals"* to the bishop and 10 marks to you, and, if you agree, I should like the vicarage to be given to some relative of R[oger] of Ingham, your brother monk, who was my partner on that journey to Rome and shared the same dangers in that cause.' At these words we all rose and thanked him, and the clerk Hugh, brother of Roger, was appointed to the church, and an annual payment of 10 marks was assigned to us.

Disputes with Canterbury

A MURDER occurred in the manor of [Monks] Eleigh, which belongs to the monks of Canterbury and is in our abbot's hundredal jurisdiction. The archbishop's men would not permit the murderers to be tried in St Edmund's court. But the abbot complained to King Henry that Archbishop Baldwin [1184–90] was laying claim to the liberties of our church,* on the strength of a recent charter given by the king to the church of Canterbury after the death of St Thomas [Becket, 1170]. The king replied that he had never issued any charter prejudicial to our church, nor did he wish to rob St Edmund of anything he had customarily possessed.*

When he heard this the abbot told his personal advisers, 'The best course would be to have the archbishop sue me rather than I sue him. I intend to take possession of the liberty and then defend myself with the help of St Edmund, to whom it rightfuly belongs, as our charters testify.' So Robert of Cockfield organized an early-morning raid, in which eighty armed men were sent to Eleigh to take the three murderers unawares. They bound and brought them back to St Edmund's, and threw them into the deepest dungeon.

When the archbishop brought his suit, the justiciar, Ranulph de Glanville, ordered that the men should be bound by securities to stand trial in the correct court, and the abbot was summoned to the king's court to answer for his use of force and the injury which he was alleged to have done to the archbishop['s rights]. The abbot appeared in person several times, and did not formally absent himself.

Finally, at the beginning of Lent [February 1187], the two parties appeared in the king's presence in the chapter-house at Canterbury, and the charters of the two churches were read out. The king commented, 'These charters are of equal antiquity and were issued by the same king, Edward [the Confessor, 1042–66]. I do not know what to say except that the documents themselves are in conflict.' To which the abbot replied, 'Whatever the charters say, we are in possession and have been down to this time. I wish to entrust my suit to the sworn statement of the two county courts of Norfolk and Suffolk that they concede this to be the case.' But Archbishop Baldwin, after some discussion with his advisers, said that the men of Norfolk and Suffolk were devoted to St Edmund, and that a large area of both counties was under the abbot's command, and that therefore he was not prepared to accept their arbitration. This angered the king, and he leapt up impatiently, and on his way out he said, 'May the best man win!' So there was an adjournment, 'and the case is still *sub judice*' [Horace, *Ars Poetica*, 78].

But I was aware that some tenants of the monks of Canterbury were badly, even fatally, wounded by peasants from the village of Milden, which is situated in one of St Edmund's hundreds [Babergh]. Now because they knew that the plaintiff had to take his case to the defendant's court, and they had absolutely no desire to plead in St Edmund's court, they preferred to stay silent and conceal the affair, rather then take their complaint to the abbot or his bailiff.

Later [1190–1] the men of Eleigh erected a weighbeam for deciding cases of false measures of bread and grain. The abbot complained about this to the bishop of Ely [William de Longchamps], who was justiciar and chancellor at that time [1189–97],* but as it was rumoured that he was sniffing after the then vacant archbishopric, he did not wish to hear the abbot's suit. However, when he stayed at our monastery as legate [at some time between June 1190 and spring 1192], before he left he prayed at the holy martyr's shrine, and while many people were listening, the abbot took the opportunity to say, 'My lord bishop, the liberty that the Canterbury monks are claiming belongs by right to St Edmund, whose body lies here. Since you will not help me to protect his church's liberty, I consider this to be a dispute between you and him. From now on he must look after his own rights.' The chancellor did not condescend to reply, and within a year he suffered the divine vengeance, and was forced to leave England [October 1191].*

On his return from Germany [spring 1193], he landed at Ipswich and spent the night at Hitcham, and a report reached the abbot that he intended to come through St Edmund's, and would hear Mass with us on the following day. So the abbot prohibited celebration of the divine office while the chancellor was present in the church, explaining that in London he had heard that the bishop of London [Richard Fitz Neal, 1189–98] had pronounced the chancellor to be excommunicate, and that he had been excommunicated in the presence of six bishops before he left England, for having used violence against the archbishop of York at Dover [September 1191].* So when the chancellor came the next day, there was no one—neither secular clerk nor monk—who would say Mass for him. Indeed, the priest who was celebrating the first Mass, and had just reached the canon of the Mass,* stopped abruptly, as did the other priests at their altars, and they all stood with their lips closed until a messenger told them that he had left the church. The chancellor pretended not to notice any of this, and brought many troubles upon the abbot before friends persuaded them to exchange the kiss of peace.

Examples of Samson's courage— an illegal tournament

WITHIN a month of taking the Cross [January 1188],* King Henry came to our church to pray. Secretly, the abbot made himself a cross of linen, and holding it in one hand, together with needle and thread, he asked the king's permission to take the Cross. But Bishop John of Norwich saw to it that permission was refused, on the grounds that it would not be in the country's best interests and would endanger the security of the counties of Norfolk and Suffolk, if both the bishop of Norwich and the abbot of St Edmund's should go away at the same time.

When it became known in London that King Richard had been taken captive and imprisoned in Germany [1192],

the barons met to consider what was to be done. Before
them all, the abbot jumped up and said that he was
prepared to search for his lord the king, either in secret or
otherwise, until he found him and identified him for
certain.* This speech was received with acclamation.

The chancellor, that is to say the bishop of Ely, held a
council at London [in October 1190] in his capacity as papal
legate, and put forward decrees against the black monks.*
He complained of their gadding about on the pretext of
pilgrimages to the shrines of St Thomas [Becket] and St
Edmund, and he criticized the abbots, confining them to a
fixed number of horses. Abbot Samson answered him, 'We
shall not accept any decree that is contrary to the Rule of St
Benedict, which allows abbots complete control over their
monks. My task is to protect the Barony of St Edmund and
his rights: thirteen horses are sufficient for some other
abbots, but not for me, as I need more in the essential
administration of royal justice.'

In the civil war that occurred throughout all England
during King Richard's captivity [1192–4], the abbot, acting
with the convent, solemnly excommunicated all those who
were responsible for violence and conflict, and was not
afraid of Count John [of Mortain], the king's brother, or
anybody else: for this reason he was said to be intrepid.
After this he went to the siege of Windsor [February–March
1193],* where he wore armour, along with some other
English abbots, and appeared with his own standard,*
leading many knights—which was a very costly operation,
although he gained more fame for his advice than for his
chivalry. But we cloister monks considered this a dangerous
proceeding, and were alarmed that as a result a future abbot
might be compelled to go on a military campaign in person.
When a truce had been arranged at that time [late March
1193], the abbot went to Germany and visited the king,
taking many gifts with him.

After King Richard's return to England [13 March 1194],

permission was given for tournaments to be held [22 August 1194].* Many knights assembled for this purpose at a site between Thetford and St Edmund's, and although the abbot forbade them, they disobeyed and carried out their intention. Some time later, eighty fully armed young men, sons of noble lords, returned to the same place with their followers to have their revenge, and came to this town afterwards to find lodging. When the abbot heard of their coming he had the town gates barred, so as to shut them all in. The next day was the eve of the Feast of SS Peter and Paul [28 June 1195], so that day, when they had given their word that they would not leave the town without permission, they were all entertained to dinner by the abbot. But after the meal, when the abbot had gone to his lodgings, they all became excited, and began dancing and singing. They sent out to the town for wine, and their drinking was followed by noisy whooping, which deprived the abbot and convent of their afternoon sleep. They did all they could to ridicule the abbot, ignoring his order to stop and persisting in their misbehaviour until evening. Then they broke the bars on the gates and got out of the town by force. The abbot, therefore, on the advice of Archbishop Hubert [Walter],* then justiciar, solemnly excommunicated them all. Afterwards many of them came to make amends, and sought absolution.

Disputes over property and rights—Jocelin's list of churches

THE abbot frequently sent his messengers to Rome on important business. Immediately after his blessing as abbot they were dispatched to obtain general confirmations of all the liberties and customs that had been granted to his predecessors, even in times of schism. Later [1187], he was the first of the English abbots to secure the right to give solemn episcopal blessing wherever he was: he obtained this for his successors as well as for himself. Later still [1188], he procured for himself and his successors general exemption from all archbishops of Canterbury: this right had been acquired by his predecessor Abbot Hugh, but only for himself.* Abbot Samson succeeded in getting included in the confirmations several new liberties which enhanced our church's independence and security. When a clergyman came to him with a letter requesting an ecclesiastical living, he took out of his document-chest seven papal letters, with bulls hanging from them. 'Look at these papal letters', he said. 'Here are requests from different popes that various clerks be given ecclesiastical benefices. I shall give you a living when I have satisfied the ones who applied ahead of you, because the man who arrives first at the mill ought to be the first to grind his corn.'

A general summons was issued in Risbridge hundred for the hearing at Wickhambrook of the claim made by [Richard] earl of Clare,* who came surrounded by numerous barons and knights, and supported by Earl Aubrey [de Vere]* and many others. Clare said that he understood from the administrators of his estates that they used to receive on his behalf 5s. a year from the hundred and its bailiffs, but that this sum was now being wrongfully withheld. He alleged that at the Conquest his predecessors had been given the land of Alfric son of Wihtgar, who had been the former lord of the hundred.* But the abbot, mindful of his rights and not willing to give anything away, replied, 'I am greatly surprised, my lord, by what you say. Your case is very weak. King Edward gave this whole hundred to St Edmund and confirmed it by charter, never mentioning these 5s. You must tell us for what service or other reason you are asking the 5s. in question.' The earl consulted his men, and then answered that it was because he had the right to carry St Edmund's banner in the army that he was owed the 5s. To this the abbot replied, 'My

word! It seems degrading that a great man like the earl of
Clare should receive so small a reward for the performance
of such a service. It would cause the abbot of St Edmund's
very little trouble to pay 5s. But Earl R[oger] Bigod*
maintains that he holds the office of St Edmund's standard-
bearer, and he fulfilled it at the time of the earl of
Leicester's capture and the Flemings' defeat [1173]; and
Thomas de Mendham also says that the office belongs to
him.* Therefore, when you have established your right
against the others, I will gladly pay you the 5s. you ask.'
Then the earl replied that he would discuss it with Earl
R[oger], who was his kinsman, and thus the case was
adjourned, and remains so to this day.

On the death of Robert of Cockfield [1190], his son Adam
came, accompanied by his relatives, by Earl Roger Bigod,
and by many other important people. They petitioned the
abbot about Adam's property, and especially about his
holding the half hundred of Cosford for an annual payment
of 100s., as if it were his inheritance, saying that his father
and grandfather had held it for more than eighty years. But
when the abbot had the opportunity to speak, he pointed
with his fingers to his eyes and said, 'May I lose these eyes
on the instant if I ever make a hundred the subject of a
hereditary grant to anyone, unless the king, who has the
power to deprive me of the abbacy, and even of my life,
forcibly compels me to do so.' He went on to explain the
reason: 'If anyone were to hold a hundred by hereditary
right, and were to be disinherited for any offence against
the king, the sheriff of Suffolk and the royal bailiffs would
immediately seize the hundred and exercise their power
within our boundaries: if they were to have custody of one
hundred, the Liberty of the eight and a half would be
jeopardized.' Then turning to speak to Adam, he said, 'If
you, who claim a hereditary interest in this hundred, should
marry a free woman with a holding of as much as one acre
directly from the king, then after your death the king would

take all your estate and the guardianship of your son, if he
should be under age, and so the king's bailiffs would enter
St Edmund's hundred, which would be injurious to the
abbot's rights. Furthermore, your father acknowledged to
me [in 1188] that he had no hereditary claim to the
hundred, and I allowed him to hold it for his lifetime as a
fitting reward for the good service he gave me.' After the
abbot's speech a large amount of money was offered him,
but he could not be persuaded either by prayers or presents.
Finally [in November 1191], they came to an agreement
whereby Adam renounced his claim in the hundred, and
the abbot confirmed to him all his other lands. But our
village of Cockfield was not mentioned, and it is believed
that he has no charter for it. He holds Semer and Groton
for his lifetime.*

When the abbot heard that Herbert the dean had built a
windmill on Haberdon,* he boiled with fury and could
hardly eat or speak. The following day, after Mass, he told
the sacrist to get his carpenters there without delay to
demolish it and store the timber in a secure place. On
receiving news of this, the dean came to say that he was
quite within his rights to act as he had on his freehold land,
and that no one ought to be denied the use of the wind. He
maintained that he had intended to grind only his own grain
there and no one else's, so as not to be regarded as having
caused loss to neighbouring mills. Still angry, the abbot
replied, 'I am as grateful to you as if you had cut off both
my feet. By God's mouth, I shall not eat bread until your
handiwork is destroyed. You are an old man, and ought to
know that even the king and the justiciar are unable to alter
or build anything in the *banleuca* without the permission of
the abbot and convent. What on earth do you think you are
doing? It is certainly not without loss to my mills, as you
contend, because the townspeople will flock to your mill to
grind their grain as they please, and in law I shall be unable
to prevent them, because they are free men. I would not

have allowed even the cellarer's new mill to remain standing if it had not been built before I became abbot. Go away,' he cried, 'Go away. Before you get home you will hear what is going to become of your mill.' But the dean, terrified by the abbot's expression, took the advice of his son, Master Stephen, and forestalled the sacrist's labourers by having his own workmen immediately pull down the mill they had themselves built, so that when the sacrist's men arrived they found nothing to demolish.

The abbot was successful in claiming the patronage of a number of churches. He also retained some that were claimed by other people—the churches of Westley, Morningthorpe [Norf.], Brettenham [Norf.], Wendling [Norf.], Pakenham, Nowton, Bradfield in Norfolk, a moiety of the church of Boxford, and the churches of Scaldwell [Northants] and Ingate [in Beccles]. He regained for his own patronage three-quarters of the church of Dickleburgh [Norf.], and the property belonging to those portions he took back into free alms,* with the exception of the land for which we owe service to the manor of Tivetshall [Norf.]. When the church of Boxford was vacant, and an inquest was summoned to decide about it,* five knights came and tried out the abbot by asking him what they should say on oath. But he would not give or promise them anything, saying, 'When it comes to your oath, speak the truth as you know it.' They went off angrily, and by their sworn statements about the last presentation they caused him to lose the patronage of that church, though he recovered it later, after incurring much expense and the payment of 10 marks.

The abbot held on to the church of Honington, which was not vacant, but was claimed by Durand de Hostesli, who showed, in support of his right, a charter of W[illiam de Turba], bishop of Norwich [1146–74], in which it is stated that Robert of Valognes, Durand's father-in-law,* gave the church to Arnold Luvel.

When half the church of Hopton became vacant [before 1190], a dispute arose between the abbot and Robert de Ulmo over the presentation for that turn. A date was arranged for a settlement at Hopton, and after much wrangling, the abbot—I cannot say what moved him to speak thus—said to Robert, 'If you will say on oath that it is rightfully yours, I will accept that it is so.' When the knight refused to swear, the consent of both parties was obtained for the question to be put to a panel of sixteen suitors of the hundred: they said on oath that the abbot had the right of presentation. Gilbert son of Ralph and Robert of Cockfield, the lords of the fee, who were present, agreed that this was correct. Then Master Jordan de Ros* sprang up, holding out two charters, one from Abbot Hugh and the other from Robert de Ulmo, so that whichever party won the case, he would get the parsonage. He said that he was the parson of the whole church, and that the clergyman who had recently died had been his vicar, who had paid him an annual sum for the half in dispute. And then he displayed a charter from Archdeacon Walkelin* on this matter. The abbot was so enraged at Jordan's action that he would not again show him any friendship until, in the chapter-house at Thetford priory,* before a large gathering of clergy, Jordan, at the abbot's insistence, made an absolute and unconditional surrender of half the church into the custody of [John] the bishop [of Norwich], and abandoned any hope of recovering it. When this was done, the abbot said, 'My lord bishop, I must keep my word to give a living to one of your clerks, so I will give this half church to whichever of your men you wish.' The bishop then suggested that it would be an amicable solution to give it to Master Jordan himself, and accordingly, on the abbot's presentation, Jordan accepted it.

Later, a dispute arose between the abbot and the same Jordan over whether the land of Herard in Harlow [Essex] was or was not held in free alms. When a jury of twelve knights was summoned in an inquest in the royal court,* the justiciar Ranulph de Glanville gave permission for it to be carried out in the abbot's court at Harlow. The jurors swore that they had never known the ownership of the disputed land to be separate from the church, but that the abbot was owed the same service for the land as was due from the holdings of Eustace and some other lay tenants in the village. The final agreement was as follows:* Master Jordan acknowledged in open court that the land was lay fee and that he had no claim in it except by the abbot's gift, and he will hold the land until the day of his death, for a quit-rent to the abbot of 12*d*. a year.

There is an English tradition by which every year on the day of Our Lord's Circumcision [1 January], the abbot, as lord, is presented with gifts by a great many people. So I, Jocelin, considered what I would give him. Then I began to write down the names of all the churches which belong to the abbot, both in our manors and in his, and I added the reasonable rents at which they could be leased, assuming an average price for grain.* At the beginning of the following year, I offered this list as my gift to the abbot, for which he was exceedingly grateful. While I was regarded by him with favour, I thought to myself that I would suggest to him that he give a church to the convent for the hospitality fund. When he had been a poor cloister monk he had wished that this might be done, and before his election had wanted the brothers to swear that whoever became abbot would see that it was carried out.* But as I considered it, I remembered that someone had raised the matter with him on an earlier occasion, and that I had heard the abbot's reply. He had said that he could not carve up the Barony, nor would it be right for him to reduce the authority and liberty that Abbot Hugh and his other predecessors had possessed over the bestowal of churches, and that they had given virtually none to the convent. So I held my tongue. This is the list I wrote:

Churches in the abbot's manors and socages:*

[Long] Melford, worth £40; Chevington, 10 marks; Saxham, 12 marks; Hargrave, 5 marks; Brettenham, 5 marks; Boxford, 100s.; Fornham [All Saints], 100s.; Stow [?West or Langtoft], 100s.; Honington, 5 marks; Elmswell, 3 marks; Cotton, 12 marks; Brockford, 5 marks; Palgrave, 10 marks; Horringer, 5 marks; Coney Weston, 4 marks; Harlow [Essex], 19 marks; Stapleford [Abbotts, Essex], 3 marks; Tivetshall [Norf.], 100s.; Worlingworth, with Bedingfield, 20 marks; [Monk] Soham, 6 marks; moiety of Wortham, 100s.; Runcton [Norf.], 20 marks; 'Thorpe', 6 marks; Woolpit, in addition to the pension, 100s.; Rushbrooke, 5 marks; moiety of Hopton [near Fakenham], 60s.; Rickinghall, 6 marks; three quarters of Dickleburgh [Norf.], 30s. and more; moiety of Gislingham, 4 marks; Icklingham, 6 marks; Mildenhall, which is worth 40 marks, and the moiety of Wetherden—what shall I say about these?* Wendling [Norf.] 100s.; [King's] Lynn [Norf.], 10 marks; Scaldwell [Northants], 5 marks; Warkton [Northants] [blank].

Churches in the convent's manors:

Mildenhall, [Great] Barton, and Horringer, 25 marks in addition to the pension; Rougham, 15 marks in addition to the pension; Bradfield [Combust], 5 marks; Pakenham, 30 marks; Southery [Norf.], 100s.; Risby, 20 marks; Nowton, 4 marks; Whepstead, 14 marks; Fornham St Genevieve, 15 marks; Herringswell, 9 marks; Fornham St Martin, 3 marks; Ingham, 10 marks; Lackford, 100s.; Elveden, 10 marks; Cockfield, 20 marks; Semer, 12 marks; Groton, 5 marks; moiety of Fressingfield, 14 marks; Beccles, 20 marks; Brooke [Norf.], 15 marks; Hinderclay, 10 marks; Warkton [Northants], 10 marks; Scaldwell [Northants] 5 marks; Westley, 5 marks; our church [St Laurence] in Norwich, 2 marks in addition to the pension of herrings; two churches in Colchester, 3 marks in addition to the pension of 4s.; Chelsworth, 100s.; Morningthorpe [Norf.], 4 marks; a moiety of Bradfield in Norfolk, 3 marks; staffacres and foracres,* and three quarters of the demesne tithes of Wrabness [Essex], 6 marks.

Samson and his knights 1196–1197

THE two counties of Norfolk and Suffolk were fined by the king's itinerant justices for an offence: 50 marks was levied on Norfolk and 30 marks on Suffolk. When a proportion of the common fine was assessed on St Edmund's lands, and then forcefully requested, the abbot went straight to the king [in 1186 or 1187], whom we found at Clarendon [Wilts.]. On being shown King Edward [the Confessor]'s charter, which freed St Edmund's lands from all taxes and payments to the Crown, the king issued written orders for six knights from the county of Norfolk and six from Suffolk to be summoned to give evidence before the Barons of the Exchequer,* as to whether St Edmund's demesnes should be exempt from common fines. To save trouble and expense, only six knights were selected, and for that reason they were landowners in both counties: Hubert of Braiseworth, W[illiam] son of Hervey, William de Francheville, and three others. They went with us to London, and on behalf of the two counties they formally attested our church's liberty, and the presiding judges enrolled their verdict.

Abbot Samson became involved in a contest with his knights, in which he was at loggerheads with them all. He was determined that they should perform the full service of fifty knights in scutages, aids, and similar levies, saying that this figure corresponded with the number of fees they held. Why, he asked, should ten knights of the fifty owe no service to him, and what was the justification or authority for the forty receiving the service of the ten? Their unanimous reply was that it was the custom for the ten always to assist the forty, and on this matter they neither would nor should be required to answer, nor be brought to court. Therefore, when they had been summoned to answer on this matter in the king's court, some purposely excused themselves, and those who did appear stated deceitfully that they would not reply without their peers. On a later occasion, when those who had previously absented themselves did attend, they made a similar statement: they would not answer because their peers, who were also concerned in the case, were not present.

After they had made the abbot look foolish several times in this way, and put him to the trouble of paying out a great deal in expenses, he made an appeal to Archbishop H[ubert Walter], who was then justiciar [December 1193–July 1198]. The archbishop's reply, given in a full council, was that each knight ought to speak for himself and his own holding. He said openly that the abbot had both the knowledge and the power to establish his church's rights against all and sundry. For this reason, Earl R[oger] Bigod became the first freely to acknowledge that in law he owed the abbot, as his lord, the full service of three knights in reliefs, scutages, and aids, but he did not mention guard duty at Norwich castle.* After this, two of the knights came, and then three, and later many more, until finally almost all had followed the earl's example in recognizing that they owed the service. But because it was not enough to acknowledge this in St Edmund's court, the abbot took them all to London at his own expense, with their wives and those women who were heiresses to estates, to make their acknowledgement in the king's court, and they each received a copy of their own agreement with the abbot [1196–7].* [Earl] Aubrey de Vere, William de Hastings, and two others were on the king's service overseas at the time of these events, so that it was necessary to postpone the case concerning them. Aubrey de Vere was the last to hold out against the abbot, but the abbot impounded and sold his cattle, so that he was obliged to come to court and answer like the others. Having taken advice, he finally acknowledged that St Edmund and the abbot were in the right. This triumph over all the knights means that unless the abbot chooses to exempt any of them, he stands to increase his income as follows: whenever scutage is levied at 20s., the abbot will make a profit of £12, and if scutage is less or more he will have proportionately less or more.

The abbot and his predecessors always used to pay 7s. out of their own account every twenty weeks for guard duty at Norwich castle. This was in lieu of the service of three knights owed to St Edmund by Earl R[oger] Bigod. The custom was that each knight of the four constabularies* would pay 28d. when he took up his stint of guard duty, and 1d. to the marshal who collected the money. It was not necessary to pay more than 28d. because the ten knights of the fifth constabulary used to assist the other forty: thus they paid only 29d. of the 3s. they owed, and whereas their guard duty ought to have come round every four months, it actually rotated every twenty weeks. But now, as each knight pays the full 3s. the difference between that and the 29d. is the abbot's profit, out of which he will be able to pay the 7s. previously mentioned. Here, then, is a clear demonstration of the fulfilment of the abbot's threats on the first occasion that he took his knights' homage, as recorded above,* when each knight made a promise of 20s. but then instantly went back on it, refusing to pay him more than the £40 in all, on the grounds that the ten knights ought to assist the other forty in aids and guard duty and all similar dues. At Tivetshall [Norf.], however, there is an ancient custom, whereby a certain tenancy on the abbot's estate pays 'wait fee'* for guard duty at Norwich, at the rate of 20s. per annum, this is 5s. on each fast day of the four terms.* The abbot would dearly like to change this if he could, but as yet he has not spoken or given any inkling of this, because he is aware that there is nothing he can do about it.

The story of Henry of Essex*

I TRUST that it is not inappropriate to include the following story in this book: my aim is to spread more widely the knowledge of the blessed king and martyr. As someone of little or no importance, I would not have committed this to writing, but according to Seneca it is not presumptuous to adopt something that has been well told by someone else [cf. *Epp.*, xii. 11]. Therefore I am treating as my own the story that Jocelin, our almoner (an extremely devout man and very able in word and deed), was persuaded to tell.

[The story ran as follows:] When we accompanied the abbot to Reading, we were very graciously received by the monks there, among whom Henry of Essex, who had taken vows in the abbey, ran up to meet us. He took the opportunity, when the abbot and the whole company were seated, of telling how he had been defeated in a duel,* and how and why St Edmund had thwarted him at the very moment of combat. On the abbot's instructions, I took this down, and this is what I wrote:

'It is essential to have an understanding of evil in order to avoid it, and for that reason it is worth recording the actions and aberrations of Henry of Essex, not as a model, but as a cautionary tale. To persuade by example is a helpful and painless way of correcting faults.

'While Henry's affairs flourished, he enjoyed considerable prestige among the nobility of the kingdom. He was well born, distinguished as a soldier, the king's standard-bearer, and by virtue of his power a man to be feared by all. But while other men who came from his part of the country were generous in making gifts of property and money to the church of the blessed Edmund, he not only ignored this, as if he were blind, but even used force and illegality to dispossess the church of an annual rent of 5s., which he appropriated for himself. Some time later, when a case was being prosecuted in St Edmund's court concerning the rape of a young girl, Henry came to protest that the hearing should take place in his court, because the girl had been born at Nayland, which was in his lordship. He persisted in this false claim for a long while, causing much trouble to St Edmund's court in journeys and numerous expenses.

'But the good fortune that had smiled on him in these and similar activities now intervened to bring him unending tribulation, and behind the illusion of a happy beginning worked out a sorrowful end for him. Fortune has a habit of smiling as a prelude to becoming enraged, of caressing only to deceive, and of praising in order to disparage.

'Before very long, Robert de Montfort, his kinsman and his equal in birth and manhood, defied him, denouncing him before the most eminent in the land and accusing him of treason against the king [March 1163].* He alleged that in the difficult expedition through Coleshill, on the Welsh campaign [1157], Henry had treacherously thrown down the king's standard, crying out loudly that the king was dead, which caused those who had been coming to the king's assistance to turn and retreat. In fact, Henry of Essex had truly believed that the illustrious King Henry II had died in a Welsh ambush—and this really would have happened, but for the action of Earl Roger of Clare, a man of celebrated lineage, and even more celebrated for his military expertise. With his men he raced up, and lifting high the king's standard he encouraged and revived the entire army. Henry did not give way to Robert in the council, and completely denied the charges, so that shortly afterwards the matter came to be settled by judicial combat.

'They met at Reading, where the duel was to take place on an island not far from the abbey, and a great crowd of people came to see the outcome. Robert fought hard and courageously, striking many resounding blows, his boldness beginning to give him the upper hand over Henry, whose strength was failing. At this point Henry looked round and was astonished to see, at the water's edge, the figure of the glorious king and martyr, Edmund, dressed in armour and apparently floating in mid-air. He was looking at Henry sternly, shaking his head repeatedly, and gesturing angrily and indignantly in a threatening fashion. Henry saw that there was with him a knight called Gilbert de Ceriville, who seemed to be lower in rank, and head and shoulders shorter [than the Saint]: he was staring at Henry, his eyes full of fury. This was a man who, on Henry's orders, had been put in chains and tortured to death, all because of an accusation by Henry's wife, who had projected her own evil thoughts on to a blameless man, saying that she was unable to withstand Gilbert's passionate demands for illicit love.

'The sight of these two alarmed and frightened Henry, and he recollected that wickedness in the past leads to shame in the present. So becoming quite desperate, he turned to attack, abandoning defence in favour of aggression. But the more powerfully he struck out, the more powerfully he was himself struck, and the more vigorously he attacked, the more vigorously was he attacked. In short, he was defeated and fell to the ground. He was taken for dead, and at the earnest request of his relatives among the English barons, his body was given to the monks of Reading for burial. But later he began to recover, and when he was given back his health, he cleansed the stain of his earlier days by taking the monastic habit, and in his concern to beautify the long week of his dissolute life with at least one sabbath, he cultivated the study of virtue, so as to produce the fruits of happiness.'

The Bishop of Ely tricked

THE bishop of Ely, Geoffrey Ridel [1174–89], asked the abbot for timber to be used in the construction of some large buildings at Glemsford. Although the abbot was reluctant to grant this, he did so for fear of offending the bishop. Then, when he was staying at Melford [Long Melford], one of the bishop's clerks came with his master's request that the promised wood should be taken from Elmswell. But 'Elmswell' was a slip of the tongue for 'Elmset', which is the name of a wood at Melford.* The abbot was surprised at this message, for Elmswell could not supply that sort of timber. However, when Richard the forester of Melford heard about it, he told the abbot privately that the previous week the bishop had sent his carpenters to Elmset as spies, and that they had selected the best trees in the whole wood and put their marks on them. Hearing this, and realizing that the bishop's messenger had made an error, the abbot answered that he was happy to agree to the bishop's request. The following day, after the messenger had left, and as soon as the abbot had heard Mass, he went with his carpenters into the wood, and ordered that all the marked oaks, and over a hundred more, should be marked again, this time with his own sign, for St Edmund, and should be felled without delay for use at the top of the great tower. When the bishop understood from his messenger that the timber was to be taken from Elmswell, he reprimanded him severely and sent him back to the abbot to correct 'Elmswell' to 'Elmset'. But before the man reached the abbot, all the trees that the bishop had desired, and his carpenters had marked, had already been felled. If his lordship wanted timber, he would have to find other trees elsewhere. When I heard this, I laughed and said to myself, 'This is an example of a trick being trumped.'

Relations with the town and the London merchants

AFTER Abbot Hugh's death, the custodians of the abbacy wanted to dismiss the reeves of St Edmund's town* and replace them with their own nominees, claiming that this right belonged to the king when the abbacy was in his hands [November 1180–February 1182]. But we made a complaint about this, and sent our messengers to Ranulph de Glanville, who was then justiciar. He replied that he knew quite well that the town owed an annual payment of £40 to our sacristy for the lighting of the church. He also said that Abbot Hugh had appointed his own candidates as reeves whenever he chose, acting on his own authority in his chamber, without the consent of the convent, but always safeguarding the payment of £40 to the altar. Therefore it should be no cause for surprise that the king's servants now required the same right on the king's behalf. He spoke severely, calling us all simpletons to have allowed our abbot to act in this fashion, but he did not take into account that the supreme obligation of monks is to keep silence and close their eyes to the aberrations of their superiors. Nor did he consider that we are called obstructive if we criticize anything, whether justly or unjustly, and that from time to time we are found guilty of disobedience and imprisoned or exiled. Therefore it seems to me and my fellows that it is wiser to die as confessors than as martyrs. When our messenger returned and gave a first-hand report of what had happened, we felt compelled to take the decision to dismiss the old town reeves, if we could, as the agreed policy of both convent and custodians, although Samson the subsacrist was against this.

When Samson became abbot, however, he remembered the injury that the convent had suffered, and on the Easter Monday after his election [i.e. 29 March 1182], he called together in our chapter-house the knights, clerks, and a crowd of burgesses, and told them all that the [revenue from the] town belonged to the convent and to the altar, for the provision of lighting in the church, and that he wanted to revive the old custom whereby the office of town reeve and associated matters belonging to the convent were dealt

with in the presence of the convent and with its common
consent. There and then two burgesses were appointed as
reeves, Godfrey and Nicholas, and after a dispute about
who should hand them the horn, called the 'Mothorn',*
they eventually received it from the prior, who, after the
abbot, is the head of the convent.

These two reeves occupied their office peacefully for
many years until they were accused of having been lax in
maintaining royal justice. After their dismissal, the abbot
ordered that Hugh the sacrist should take the town into his
custody, in order to safeguard the convent's interests. He
appointed new officers to answer to him in the performance
of their duties. But in the course of time, I do not know
how, new reeves were appointed outside the chapter meeting and without the convent's agreement. Consequently
there is concern that after the death of Abbot Samson there
will be a similar or greater threat than after Abbot Hugh's
death.

One of our brother monks, who was quite sure of the
abbot's affection and friendship, went to him, as soon as he
had a chance, and tactfully told him that there was grumbling in the convent. On hearing this the abbot was silent
for a long while, as if rather put out, and was reported to
have answered at last, 'Surely I, and I only, am abbot? Is it
not my business to deal with the affairs of the church which
is in my charge, at least so long as I have my wits and act
according to God's will? If there is any failure of royal
justice in this town, it is I who will be blamed, and I who
will be summoned; it is I who will bear the burden of travel
and expense, as well as of the defence of the town and
similar responsibilities. It is I who will be thought stupid,
not the prior, not the sacrist, not the convent, but I alone,
because I am their head—or ought to be. It is through me
and my policy, with God's help and to the best of my
ability, that the town shall be preserved without loss and
the annual £40 due to the altar secured. The brothers can

grumble and criticize and talk among themselves as much as they like: I am their father and their abbot. I shall not hand over my position to anyone else, so long as I live.' At this the monk left him, and reported the abbot's reply. I found the words perplexing, and debated the pros and cons to myself, but in the end I was forced to remain doubtful, because canon law says and teaches that everything is in the abbot's control.*

The merchants of London wished to be free from the payment of toll at St Edmund's market, and many of them paid it unwillingly and under pressure. This issue provoked a great storm and outcry among the Londoners in their hustings-court, and they then came and told Abbot Samson that they were entitled to freedom from payment throughout England on the authority of a charter they had received from King Henry II.* The abbot replied to this that, if necessary, he could quite well call on the king to warrant that he had never given any charter prejudicial to our church's interests, nor detrimental to St Edmund's Liberty, to which, before the Norman Conquest, St Edward [the Confessor] had granted and confirmed toll and team and all regalian rights.* He said that King Henry had given the Londoners freedom from toll throughout his own demesnes, where he had the power to do so, but in St Edmund's town he could not, because it did not belong to him. When the Londoners heard this, they resolved in common council that none of them would go to St Edmund's market, and they kept away for two years, as a result of which our market was hard hit and the payments to the sacristy were very considerably reduced. Eventually, through the mediation of the bishop of London and many others, a settlement was reached whereby they would come to the market, and some of them would pay toll, but would immediately receive it back, so that by this pretence the rights of both parties would be preserved.

But some time later, when the abbot had come to an

agreement with his knights [1196–7], and everything seemed to be tranquil, suddenly the cry went up again, 'The Philistines be upon thee, Samson!' [Judg. 16:9, 12, 14, 20]. The Londoners were threatening to pull down the stone houses that the abbot had built that year, or else take a hundredfold distraint* on the men of St Edmund, unless the abbot quickly put right the harm that had been done them by the reeves of St Edmund's town, who had made a charge of 15*d.* on the Londoners' carts which carried herrings through the town on their way from Yarmouth. They claimed that as citizens of London they had been free from toll at all times and in all places, in every market-place throughout all England, ever since the foundation of Rome. The city of London had been founded at the same time, and ought to have this freedom throughout all England, because of its privileged status as a former metropolis* and as the kingdom's capital, and also because of its antiquity. The abbot requested that the dispute be suspended until the king should return to England, so that he could take his advice, and after he had consulted the lawyers, he repaid the 15*d.* to the claimants, without prejudice to the rights of either side.

In the tenth year of Abbot Samson's abbacy [1191–2], we agreed in our chapter to take a complaint to the abbot in his court. We said that although the rents and revenues of all the better towns and boroughs in England were on the increase, to the advantage of those who possessed them and to the profit of the landlords, this town was an exception, as it customarily yielded £40 and never produced any more. We maintained that the burgesses of the town were responsible for this state of affairs: they had made very many sizeable encroachments in the market-place, in shops, booths, and stalls, without the convent's permission, and on the sole authority of the town reeves, who paid a fixed annual sum to the sacrist, as if they were his officials, and could be dismissed at his pleasure.

When the burgesses were summoned, they replied that they were in the king's protection, and on the question of their holdings, which they and their fathers had held for a year and a day, satisfactorily, peacefully, and without trouble, they refused to answer, as that would be contrary to the liberty of the town and their charters. They said that the ancient custom was that, without consulting the convent, the reeves granted sites of shops and booths in the market-place, for an annual rent to be paid to them. But we protested loudly, asking the abbot to dispossess them of those holdings for which they had no warrant.

The abbot came to our council, as if he were one of us, and told us confidentially that he wanted to do all in his power to see that we retained our rights, but that he had to act according to judicial process, and without a court judgement he could not dispossess free men of lands or rents which, rightly or wrongly, they had held for a period of years. He said that if he were to do that, he would be liable to punishment by the king, according to the law of the land.

The burgesses, therefore, agreed among themselves to offer the convent a payment of 100s., to end the dispute and ensure that they might continue in their holdings as before. But we would not allow this, preferring to postpone the case in the hope that under another abbot we might either recover everything or change the site of the market, and so the matter was deferred for several years.

When Abbot Samson returned from Germany [1193], the burgesses offered him 60 marks and asked him to confirm the town's liberties in the same terms as the confirmation charters of his predecessors, Anselm, Ording, and Hugh, and he generously agreed to this. While we grumbled and groaned, the charter was written out as he had promised them,* and as it would have been humiliating and embarrassing for him to be unable to carry out his promise, we did not like to object or provoke his anger. Once the burgesses laid hands on the charter of Abbot Samson and the convent, they were very confident that so long as he was abbot they would never lose their holdings or their liberties, and consequently from that time forward they never gave or offered the payment of 100s. which they had made previously. But the abbot eventually noticed this, and summoned the burgesses to tell them that if they did not come to an agreement with the convent, he would forbid them to put up their booths at St Edmund's market. They replied that each year they would give a silk cope or other precious item worth 100s., as they had promised previously, but only on condition that they should forever be free from the payment of tithing-pence,* which the sacrist used assiduously to demand from them. But the abbot and the sacrist were opposed to this, and so the matter was again deferred. Indeed, we have lost those 100s. right down to the present time: as the saying goes, 'He who is slow to profit when he may, will be unable to do so when he chooses.'

The cellarer in debt

CELLARERS succeeded one another in rapid succession, and at the end of the year each one of them was deep in debt. To assist the cellarer, £20 was given him from Mildenhall, but this was insufficient. Then an annual sum of £50 was allotted to the cellarer from the same manor, and still he said it was not enough. The abbot, therefore, wishing to ensure that neither he nor we should suffer any loss or disadvantage, and knowing that whenever we were in financial trouble we turned to him as father of the monastery, appointed a clerk from his own circle, called Master Ranulph,* to act in partnership with our cellarer, and to help him as a witness and colleague in dealing with both income and expenditure.

This caused a good deal of talk. The air grew thick with

complaints, lies were invented, slander was added to slander, and no corner of the monastery was free from the
sound of poisonous whisperings. One man said to another,
'What on earth has happened? Whoever saw the like?
Never has the convent been so disgraced. Look how the
abbot has appointed a clerk over a monk! A clerk! to be
director and supervisor over the cellarer, so that no action
may be taken without him! The abbot despises his monks
and treats them with suspicion, but clerks he consults and
values. "How is the gold become dim! How is the finest
lustre changed!" [Lam. 4:1].' Likewise, friend said to
friend, '"We are become a reproach to our neighbours"
[Ps. 79:4]. We monks are all considered to be either
unreliable or lacking in foresight. A clerk is trusted, but
not a monk. The abbot has more confidence in a clerk than
a monk. Is that clerk more reliable or wiser than any
monk?' Colleague said to colleague, 'Surely the cellarer and
subcellarer are, or may be, no less trustworthy than the
sacrist or the chamberlain? The consequence of this action
is that the present abbot or his successors may put a clerk
with the sacrist, a clerk with the chamberlain, a clerk with
the subsacrists for collecting the offerings at the shrine,
and, in the same way, a clerk with every official, so that we
shall be held in "scorn and derision" [Ps. 44:13] by the
entire population.'

When I heard this kind of conversation, I used to answer,
'If I were cellarer, I should be very glad to have a clerk
witness everything I did, because if I did well, he would
provide evidence of it, but if at the end of the year I was in
debt, my word might be accepted and I might be exonerated
on the clerk's testimony.' But I heard one of our most
discerning and educated brothers say something that
impressed me and many others. 'It is not surprising', he
said, 'that the abbot puts in his own men to look after our
affairs, because he is a good administrator of that part of
the abbey that belongs to him, and manages his household

wisely, and it is he who would have to make up any loss on our side if it arose from our carelessness or failure. But,' he went on, 'after Abbot Samson's death there lurks a danger that has never occurred in our lifetime. The king's bailiffs will surely come and take the abbacy—that is, the abbot's Barony—into their hands, as happened in the past, after the death of other abbots. After Abbot Hugh's death, the king's bailiffs sought to appoint new reeves in the town of St Edmund, claiming that they had the right because Abbot Hugh had done the same. In the same way, in course of time, the king's bailiffs will use a similar reasoning, justifying their action by the precedent of Abbot Samson's deeds, and will appoint their clerk to look after the cellary, so that everything is done through him and on his orders. In this way the affairs and revenues of the abbot and convent, which were carefully distinguished and kept separate from one another by Abbot Robert of happy memory [1102–7],* may become intermingled and confused.' These remarks, and others in a similar vein, coming as they did from a wise and prudent man, caused me some consternation, and not wishing either to condemn or defend the abbot's action, I held my tongue.

A visitation forestalled

HUBERT WALTER, who was archbishop of Canterbury, papal legate [March 1195–January 1198], and justiciar of England, had carried out visitations of many churches, and had introduced many changes and innovations by virtue of his legatine authority, when on his return from his mother's death-bed at Dereham [West Dereham, Norf., in 1195], he sent two of his clerks to us, with a sealed letter from their master which told us that we could confide in them completely. They asked the abbot and convent whether when their master, the legate, came here we would receive him as a legate ought to be received and is received by other churches. If we were to agree to this, he would arrive quite soon to deal with the affairs of our church in consultation with the abbot and convent and according to God's will. If we were unwilling to allow it, then the two clerks would explain their master's orders more fully.

The abbot called together several from the convent, and we drew up this plan: we would make a courteous reply to the clerks who had been sent to us, saying that we would receive their master, as legate, with all honour and reverence, and we would dispatch our own messengers to go with them, to say this to the legate on our behalf. We agreed that, as we had done previously with the bishop of Ely and other legates, we would show him all honour by receiving him with a procession and the ringing of bells, and with other ceremonies, up to the moment when he might attempt a visitation in chapter. If he were to do this, we should all with one accord oppose him to his face, appeal to Rome, and put our trust in our charters. The abbot said, 'If the legate wishes to come here immediately, we shall do as we have just said. But if he postpones his visit for a while, we shall consult the pope in the meantime. We shall ask him what force those privileges that were obtained for our church from him and his predecessors should have against an archbishop who has gained power from the Holy See over all the privileged churches of England.' This was our plan.

When the archbishop heard that we were willing to receive him as legate, he gave our messengers a warm and grateful reception, and in all his dealings with the abbot he treated him with kindness and favour, postponing his visit here for a while because other matters required his attention. Therefore the abbot lost no time in forwarding to the pope the letter which the legate had sent him and the convent. This was the letter in which he announced that he intended to visit us on his authority as legate, and on papal authority, and in which it was stated that he had been given

power over all the exempt churches of England, notwith-
standing the documents obtained by the church of York*
or anyone else. At the request of the abbot's messenger, the
pope wrote to the archbishop [January 1196] telling him
that our church, as his spiritual daughter, was answerable
to no legate, except a legate *a latere* sent by the pope
himself, and he forbade him to raise his hand against us.
The pope added, of his own accord, a prohibition against
the exercise of his power in any other exempt church.*

Our messenger returned to us, and the news was kept
secret for some days. But it was revealed to the archbishop
by members of his circle who had been at the papal Curia.
So when the legate made his visitation through Norfolk and
Suffolk at the end of the year, and came first to Colchester,
he secretly sent a messenger to the abbot, telling him that
he had heard from a reliable source that the abbot had
obtained a letter against his legatine powers, and asking
him to send the letter to him as a friend. This was done, for
the abbot had an exact duplicate. But while the legate was
in the diocese of Norwich, the abbot made no approach to
him, either in person or by proxy, in case it should be
thought that he wished to come to an agreement with the
legate over our receiving him as a guest, as other monks
and canons had done. This upset and angered the legate,
and because he was afraid of being refused entrance if he
arrived here, he travelled by Norwich, Acre [Castle Acre],
and Dereham [Norf.], and crossed to [the Isle of] Ely on
his way back to London.

When, in less than a month's time [c.20 March 1197],
the abbot met the legate on the king's highway between
Waltham [Essex] and London,* the legate accused him of
refusing to meet him as king's justiciar when he was in our
part of the country. The abbot replied that he had come not
as justiciar but as legate, carrying out a visitation of every
church, and he claimed that it was an impossible time of
the year for him, with Passiontide approaching [23 March],

when he had to attend to services and monastic observances. As the abbot answered him word for word and point for point, and was not in the least intimidated or put off, the legate replied angrily that he knew well how good the abbot was at disputation, and that he was better educated than he was himself. It was not out of timidity that the abbot omitted things that ought not to be spoken, nor was it out of pomposity that he said what needed to be said, and so he replied in the hearing of many that he was not the sort of man who would ever allow the liberty of his church to be weakened through lack of knowledge or money, even if he had to die or be condemned to perpetual exile. At the end of these and similar arguments, the legate began to go red in the face, and the abbot spoke more moderarely, asking him to treat St Edmund's church more gently on account of his local birth, since he was virtually a man of St Edmund, born and bred. The legate blushed because he had unadvisedly poured out the venom that had formed within him. The following day the archbishop was told that the archbishop of York was on his way to England as legate, and that he had reported to the pope many evil things about him, saying that on his visitation he had oppressed the churches of England by taking from them 30,000 silver marks. The legate therefore sent his clerks to the abbot, asking him, along with other abbots, to write to the pope and clear his name. The abbot agreed to do this, and, speaking according to his conscience, testified that the archbishop of Canterbury had neither visited our church nor oppressed it or any other church. When the abbot handed this letter to the archbishop's messengers, he said in front of everybody that he was not afraid, even if the archbishop wished to put the letter to some evil use. In reply, the clerks gave their solemn word that their master was not seeking to deceive in any way, but simply wanted to be exonerated. So the archbishop and the abbot became friends.

Problems with knights' services overseas— Samson visits Normandy 1197

[IN 1197] King Richard commanded all the English bishops and abbots to arrange for one knight to represent every ten in their baronies, and to join him immediately in Normandy, bringing horses and weapons, to support him in his campaign against the French king.* The abbot was expected to send four knights. But when all his knights arrived in answer to his summons, they replied that the fees which they held of St Edmund did not owe service outside England, nor had they or their fathers ever gone on service abroad, but they had sometimes paid scutage on the king's orders. The abbot was put in an awkward position, since on the one hand he realized that the freedom of his knights was in danger, while on the other he was afraid of losing possession of his Barony if he failed in his service to the king, as had happened to the bishop of Lincoln* and many other English barons. So he crossed the Channel at once, but although he exhausted himself with his exertions and expenses and the very many gifts he made to the king, he was unable at first to come to any agreement with the king on the basis of money. When the king said that he did not need gold or silver, but urgently required four knights, the abbot offered four hired knights, who were accepted by the king and sent to the castle of Eu,* the abbot giving them 36 marks for expenses for forty days. The next day, however, some of the king's friends came and advised the abbot to take careful forethought, saying that the war might last a whole year or more, and the knights' expenses might increase and multiply, resulting in permanent loss to himself and his church. Therefore their advice was that before he left the court he should make an agreement with the king that his responsibility for the knights should cease after forty days. So the abbot acted on this wise advice, gave the king £100 for the agreement, and returned to

England with the king's favour, bringing a royal writ empowering him to exact from his knights' fees the sums he had paid to the king for their service. But when the knights were summoned, they offered him 2 marks for each shield, pleading poverty and many various impositions. The abbot, remembering that he had laid a charge on them that very year, and had taken them to court for their payment of scutage in full, and wishing to gain their favour, gratefully accepted what they gladly offered him.

At this time, although the abbot had incurred many expenses in his journey overseas, he did not return to his church empty-handed, but brought a golden cross and a precious gospel-book worth 80 marks. Another time when he came back from abroad, he said as he sat in chapter that if he were cellarer or chamberlain, he would do something to improve the finances of his office, but as he was abbot, he ought to acquire something worthy of an abbot. With these words, he gave the convent a precious chasuble, a mitre of cloth of gold, sandals with silk buskins, and the finely wrought silver head of a crosier.* In the same way, whenever he came home from overseas, he would bring back some precious item.

The cellarer again—unpopular reforms 1197

IN the year 1197 certain innovations and changes were made in our church, which ought not to be passed over in silence. Because our cellarer found his customary income insufficient, Abbot Samson ordered that an additional £50 per annum be given to him, to be paid by the prior. This sum was not to come to him all at once, but in monthly instalments, so that he would have an allowance to spend each month, and in this way the whole amount would not be dissipated at one time of the year. This was done for a year. But the cellarer and his associates made a complaint, saying that if he were to have all the money at once, he would make his own arrangements and supply his needs himself. The abbot reluctantly agreed to this request. By the beginning of August the cellarer had already spent it all, and was another £26 in debt, and was heading for a debt of £50 by Michaelmas.*

The abbot was annoyed to hear this, and made the following statement in chapter: 'I have often threatened that I would take over the management of your cellary, because year after year, through your failure to plan ahead, you run up great debts. I appointed my clerk to act with your cellarer as a witness, so that business might be conducted more sensibly, but there is no clerk or monk who dares explain to me the reason for the debt. Rumour has it, however, that the cause lies in extravagant entertainment in the prior's lodging, which has had the approval of prior and cellarer, and in unnecessary expenses in the guest-house, which have arisen through the guest-master's carelessness. You see,' he said, 'the large debt that looms before us: give me your advice on how matters may be put right.' Many cloister monks were glad to hear these words and half-smiled to themselves, saying in private that what the abbot had said was correct. The prior put the blame on the cellarer, and the cellarer blamed the guest-master. Each man made excuses for himself. But we knew the truth, although we were afraid to speak it.

The following day the abbot came and said again to the convent, 'Give me your advice on how your cellary may be managed more efficiently.' No one answered a word, except one man who said that in the refectory there was definitely no excess from which any debt or loss should arise. On the third day the abbot repeated his request, to which someone replied, 'This advice has to come from you, as our head.' Then the abbot said, 'Since you are unwilling to advise me, and do not know how to manage your domestic affairs, the administration of the monastery falls to me as father and chief protector.' He went on, 'I am taking the management of your cellary under my own direction, and also the hospitality fund and the organization of provisions, both our own produce and our purchases.' Having made this statement, he deposed the cellarer and the guest-master, and appointed two monks, to be called subcellarer and guest-master, attaching them to Master G., a clerk of his own,* whose approval was needed for any transaction relating either to food and drink, or to income and expenditure. The old buyers were not allowed to make the purchases in the market-place, and foodstuffs were bought by the abbot's clerk. Our losses were made up out of the abbot's money. Guests qualified to receive accommodation were given it, and those worthy of special respect were entertained with honour; monastic officials and cloister monks alike ate in the refectory, and everywhere unnecessary expenditure was reduced.

Some of the cloister monks said to one another, 'There were seven persons, just seven, who consumed our goods, but if anyone spoke of their waste, he was regarded as a traitor.' Another said, raising his hands to heaven, 'May God be blessed for having given the abbot the will to put these matters right.' And many said that what was being done was right. But others said it was not: they considered the reforms to be degrading, and they likened the abbot's discernment to the savageness of a wolf, for they remembered what had been foretold long ago in the dream, that the future abbot would rage like a wolf.

The knights and the people were baffled by what was being done, and an ordinary man said, 'It is remarkable that the monks, for all their education, tolerate their property and money being confused and merged with the abbot's, as they have always been divided and kept separate from one another. It is amazing that they do not guard against the possible danger that after the abbot's death the king might find them in that parlous state.' Another man said that the abbot was the only man who had the wisdom to organize external affairs, and that as he knew how to run everything, he ought to do so. And someone said, 'If there was even one wise monk in that great convent who knew how to run its domestic affairs, the abbot would not have acted as he has.' And so 'we became a scorn and derision to them that are round about us' [Ps. 79: 4].

During this period, the time came round for Abbot Robert's anniversary to be read out in chapter, and it was decided that the *Placebo* and *Dirige** be sung with more solemnity than usual, with ringing of the great bells, as on the anniversaries of Abbots Ording and Hugh. This was because of Abbot Robert's celebrated action in separating our property and revenues from those of the abbot. The intention of certain people was that the performance of this ceremony might, at all events, move the abbot's heart towards well-doing. There was one person, however, who thought that it was organized in order to embarrass the abbot, who, because he had taken over the management of our cellary, was said to want to confuse and merge our property and income with his own. But when the abbot heard the unexpected sound of bells, although well aware that this was contrary to normal procedure, he sensibly ignored what lay behind it, and sang Mass with all solemnity.

On the following day, which was Michaelmas [29 September], partly because he wanted to put a stop to the mutterings of certain persons, he appointed the former subcellarer to be cellarer and directed that a particular monk be nominated as subcellarer; but the aforesaid clerk was still attached to them, and was administering everything as before. Now when this clerk had too much to drink, admitting, 'I'm drunk',* he held the cellarer's court without the abbot's knowledge, took securities, received the annual rents, and spent money on his own authority, so that he was openly referred to as the chief cellarer. Frequently he would go to and fro through the courtyard, and

would be followed, as if he were master and chief administrator, by many people of various classes on different kinds
of business—rich and poor, debtors and claimants. One of
our obedientiaries, who happened to be standing in the
courtyard, wept out of embarrassment and shame on seeing
this. He brooded on both the disgrace to our church and
the possible future danger, and reflected how injurious to
the whole convent was the elevation of clerk over monk.
This man, whoever he was, arranged through an interme-
diary for these matters to be made known to the abbot
politely and calmly. In this way the abbot came to see that
such arrogance in a clerk, which was bringing shame and
dishonour on everybody, might give rise to much disorder
and dissension in the convent. So when he heard, he
immediately sent for the cellarer and the said clerk, and
ordered that in future the cellarer himself should act as
cellarer in receiving cash, hearing cases in court, and in all
other business, with the proviso that the clerk should assist,
not as an equal, but as a witness and an adviser.

A will and an excommunication 1197

[IN 1197] when Hamo Blund, one of this town's wealthier
men, was dying, he was reluctant to make any sort of will.
He finally made one which disposed of only 3 marks, and
which was witnessed by no one except his brother, wife,
and chaplain. After Hamo's death, the abbot learned of
this, and summoned these three, whom he reproached
bitterly because the brother (who was his heir) and the wife
had not permitted anyone to visit Hamo when he was ill,
wishing to take everything for themselves. The abbot said
in court: 'I was his bishop and had care of his soul. To
prevent the ignorance of his priest and confessor endanger-
ing my soul, because I was away and could not direct the
sick man while he was alive, I shall do my duty, late though
it is. My instructions are that all his debts and his movable

chattels, which are said to be worth 200 marks, should be listed, and one part should be given to his heir, another part to his wife, and the third to his poor relations and other poor people.* But I command that the horse which was led before the dead man's bier and offered to St Edmund, should be returned: for our church must not be polluted by the gift of a man who died intestate, and whom public opinion charges with having habitually lent money at interest. By God's mouth, if while I live anyone in future does the same thing, he shall not be buried in the cemetery.' Those to whom these words were directed went away stunned.

On the day after Christmas Day [1197], there were gatherings in the cemetery, with contests and competitions between the abbot's servants and the townspeople, but matters escalated from words to blows, and then from punches to wounds and bloodshed. When the abbot heard about it, he asked some of those who had gone to the show, but had stood on the sidelines, to come and see him privately, and he commanded the names of the miscreants to be written down. He had all these summoned to appear before him in St Denis's chapel on the day after St Thomas [Becket]'s Day [i.e. 30 December]. In the interim he did not invite any of the townspeople to his table as in previous years he had normally done on the first five days of Christmas. On the appointed day, after the evidence on oath of sixteen sworn men had been heard, the abbot said, 'These wicked men obviously fall within the canon *sentenciae latae*, but because they are laymen from here and roundabout, and do not appreciate how outrageous it is to commit such sacrilege, I shall publicly excommunicate them by name,* so that others may be more fearful. I shall begin with my own household and servants to ensure that justice is done impartially.' This was carried out as soon as we had put on stoles and candles were lit. Then they all left the church, and after some discussion they undressed and,

naked except for their pants, prostrated themselves in front
of the church door. When the abbot's assistants, monks
and clerks, came and told him tearfully that over a hundred
naked men were lying there, the abbot also wept. But in his
words and in his face he displayed the severity of the law,
hiding his inner compassion, for he wished to be urged by
his advisers to absolve the penitents, knowing that mercy is
exalted above judgement, and that the church receives all
those who repent. Therefore, when they had all been
severely beaten and absolved, they took an oath that they
would accept the church's judgement regarding the sacrilege they had committed. The following day they were
given penances according to canon law, and the abbot took
them all back into complete unity. But he uttered terrible
threats against anyone who, by word or deed, should create
discord, and he publicly prohibited assemblies and shows
in the cemetery. So, when everyone had been restored to
the blessing of peace, it was with great rejoicing that on the
following days the townspeople feasted with their lord the
abbot.

More reforms—new buildings and a canopy for St Edmund's shrine

[IN 1197] the pope commissioned Hubert [Walter], archbishop of Canterbury, [Hugh of Avallon] the bishop of
Lincoln, and Abbot Samson of St Edmund's to reform the
church of Coventry and reinstate the monks without further
inquiry.* When the parties had been called together at
Oxford, the judges received a letter from the king requesting them to adjourn the business. The archbishop and
bishop dissembled and said nothing, as if they were trying
to gain the approval of the clerks, and only the abbot spoke
out openly as a monk on behalf of the monks of Coventry,
publicly favouring and championing their cause. At his

instigation matters proceeded so far on that day that full possession was transferred to one of the monks of Coventry using a book as a symbol.* But their entry into the church was delayed for a time so that to this extent the judges might comply with the king's request. Meanwhile the abbot received in his lodgings fourteen of the Coventry monks who had come to Oxford. The monks sat at one table, and at another sat the masters of the university who had been invited. The abbot was commended for his splendid and generous hospitality. Nor did he ever seem happier in the whole of his life than he was at that time, due to his fervour for re-establishing the monastic order. With the Feast of St Hilary [13 January 1198] approaching, the abbot set out for Coventry in high spirits. He was not deterred by either the trouble or the expense, and said that even if he was forced to be carried in a litter he would not be left behind. During the five days after he had reached Coventry and before the archbishop's arrival, he gave suitable accommodation in his house to all the monks and their servants, until the new prior was appointed and the monks officially installed.

'He that hath ears to hear, let him hear' of this renowned action [Matt. 11: 15]. After the question of half the advowson of the church of Wetherden had been settled between Abbot Samson and Robert de Scales [21 April 1198],* and the rights of St Edmund and of the abbot had been recognized by Robert, the abbot, although there had been no prior arrangement or promise, gave his half of the church to Master R. de Scales, the knight's brother, on condition that he should make over to the sacrist an annual sum of 3 marks, which would be paid to whoever was teaching as master of the schools in St Edmund's town. The abbot's action was inspired by a memorable piety, and just as in the past he had bought some stone houses for the school so that poor clerks were released from paying rents, so now he freed them from all future fees which the master of the schools normally charged for tuition. So if it is the will of God and the abbot survives, the whole moiety of this church, which is said to be worth 100s., will be put to this purpose.

When the abbot had erected many different buildings in the villages throughout his estates and had stayed overnight on his manors more often than at home with us, at last he came to himself, and changing good for better, he announced that he would in future spend more time at home. He said that he would construct needed buildings within the court, paying attention to work here as well as elsewhere, acknowledging that 'the master's presence enriches the field' [Palladius I.i.6]. He ordered that the stables and outbuildings round the courtyard, which previously had been reed-thatched, were to be tiled, under the supervision of Hugh the sacrist, so that there should be no further fear or danger from fire. 'Behold, the acceptable time' [2 Cor. 6: 2]; the long-desired day has come, which as guest-master I am particularly happy to describe. See how on the abbot's orders the court echoes to the sound of pickaxes and stonemasons' tools as the guest-house is knocked down. At this very moment nearly all is demolished. May the most high God provide for the rebuilding! The abbot constructed a new larder for himself in the court, and gave the old larder, which was in an unsuitable position under the dormitory, to the convent, for the chamberlain's use. The chapels of St Andrew, St Katherine, and St Faith were newly roofed with lead. Also many improvements were made inside the church and out. If you don't believe this, open your eyes and look.

At this time, too, our almonry was rebuilt in stone— formerly it had been ramshackle and of wood. Towards this our brother Walter the physician, then almoner, gave a large donation of money that he had made from his medical practice.

In addition, the abbot, seeing that the silver frontal of the high altar and many other precious ornaments had been disposed of to pay for the recovery of Mildenhall and for King Richard's ransom, did not wish to refashion the frontal and other similar panels in case they should suffer the same fate of being stripped off and dispersed. Instead, he concentrated all his efforts on making a most precious canopy above the shrine of the glorious martyr Edmund, so that his work of art would be put in a position from which it could in no circumstances be taken down, and where no man would dare lay a hand on it. Indeed, when King Richard was a prisoner in Germany [1192–4], there was not one treasure in England that was not given or exchanged for money, and yet the shrine of St Edmund remained intact. Nevertheless, whether St Edmund's shrine should be partly stripped for the king's ransom was argued before the Barons of the Exchequer, and the abbot stood up and answered the point in this way: 'Take it for a certainty, that this shall never be authorized by me, nor is there any man who would get me to agree to it. But I will open the doors of the church—let anyone enter who will, let anyone come near who dare.' Each judge replied with an oath, 'I shall not go', 'Nor I. St Edmund vents his rage on the distant and the absent: much greater will his fury be on those close at hand who seek to rob him of his clothing.' Because of what had been said, the shrine was not despoiled, nor was a loan raised on it. So putting other matters aside, the abbot decided very wisely and sensibly to construct a canopy for the shrine. And now sheets of gold and silver resound between the hammer and the anvil, and 'craftsmen handle craftsmen's tools' [Horace, *Epistolae*, II. i. 116].

A dispute with the king 1198

WHEN Adam of Cockfield died [probably 1198], he left a daughter of three months as his heiress, and the abbot gave the wardship of her fee as he chose. King Richard, however, petitioned by some of those close to him, caused trouble by seeking the wardship and the girl for one of his courtiers, persistently sending both letters and messengers to this end. But the abbot answered that he had given the wardship and confirmed it in a charter, and sending a messenger to the king, he tried by entreaty and gift to appease the king's anger, if that was at all possible. In great indignation, the king replied that he would get his own back on this proud abbot who went against his wishes, but he held back out of reverence and fear of St Edmund. Thus when the messenger returned, the abbot shrewdly ignored the king's threats, saying, 'If he wishes, the king may send and take the ward. He has the strength and power to effect his will and take away the whole abbacy. I will never bend and do what he wishes, nor will I ever authorize it, for fear that the consequences of such an action would be to the disadvantage of my successors. I will never pay money to the king in this business. The Almighty shall see to it. Whatever happens, I shall endure it patiently.' Just when many were saying and thinking that the king was hostile towards the abbot, most surprisingly the king wrote in friendly fashion to the abbot requesting that he should give him some of his hunting dogs. The abbot, mindful of the judicious saying, 'Bribes, believe me, win both gods and men, and Jupiter himself is appeased by the offering of gifts' [Ovid, *Ars Amat.* iii. 653–4], sent dogs as the king had requested, and also horses and other valuable gifts. The king accepted these gratefully, and publicly before his earls and barons commended the abbot's probity and staunchness. [Between February 1198 and April 1199,] as a token of his friendship and affection, he sent messengers to the abbot with a precious ring which Pope Innocent III, out of his great charity, had given him, and which was the first gift made to the king after the pope's consecration [22 February 1198]; and he wrote warmly thanking the abbot for the many gifts he had received.

Changes in customs—the cellarer and his rights

MANY people were astonished at the alterations to the customs which Abbot Samson directed or allowed. Ever since the town of St Edmund had been given the name and status of a borough, men had been accustomed to pay to the cellarer, at the beginning of August, a penny on each dwelling for the cutting of our corn. This payment was called 'repsilver', because before the town gained its freedom, everyone used to do the reaping, like serfs. Only the houses of knights, chaplains, and servants of the court were exempt from the payment. In the course of time, the cellarer exempted some of the richer men of the town, exacting nothing from them. Other burgesses, seeing this, declared openly that no one who had his own messuage ought to pay the penny, but only those who rented houses. Later they all made a joint demand for this exemption, coming to the abbot and offering an annual payment instead. The abbot, indeed, considering how the cellarer went about the town in an unbecoming manner collecting 'repsilver', how he took goods from the houses of the poor as securities for payment—sometimes stools, sometimes doors, sometimes other essentials—and how little old women came out with their distaffs threatening and reproaching him and his officers, decided that 20s. should be paid to the cellarer yearly at the borough court that met just before August. This was to be rendered by the burgesses through the agency of the reeve, to whom they entrusted the money for this purpose. And thus it was done and confirmed in our charter [before c.1200].*

The burgesses were also released from a customary payment known as 'sorpeni', in return for a lump sum of 4s. to be made on the same occasion [as the above]. The cellarer had been accustomed to take a penny a year for the putting out to pasture of each cow belonging to the men of the town, unless the cows were owned by chaplains or servants of the court. He used to place the cows in a pound, and this caused a great deal of work. When the abbot first raised this subject in chapter, the convent reacted with indignant annoyance, and Benedict the subprior spoke for all when he said, 'Abbot Ording, yes, Ording, he who lies there,* would not do such a thing for 500 silver marks.' This angered the abbot, and he deferred the matter for a while.

Likewise there was a major disagreement between R[?obert] the cellarer and Hugh the sacrist over the income from their offices: the sacrist did not wish to allow the cellarer to use the town gaol for locking up thieves who were arrested on the cellarer's property. For this reason the cellarer was often given much trouble, and when robbers escaped he was blamed for failing to get justice done. It happened, too, that a certain free tenant of the cellarer, called Ketel, who lived outside the [town] gate, was charged with robbery, and after he had failed in the duel, was hanged. The convent was embarrassed by the accusations of the burgesses, who said that if the man had lived inside the town, he would not have been brought to the duel, but would have acquitted himself by the oaths of his neighbours, as is the privilege of those who live within the town. The abbot and the wiser members of the convent, understanding this, and being aware that the inhabitants both within the borough and without were subject to us, and that all ought to enjoy the same rights within the *banleuca* (except the *lancetti* of Hardwick* and men of the same status), made careful plans to bring this about. The abbot also wished to define the offices of sacrist and cellarer on certain points and settle their disputes, and seeming to favour the sacrist's side, ordered that the servants of the town reeve and the servants of the cellarer should enter the cellarer's fee together to arrest robbers and evil-doers. The town reeve should have half the sum for the imprisonment and custody of the thieves and for his labours, and the court of the cellarer should come to the borough court, and there those who were to be tried should be tried by the two courts jointly. It was also decided that the cellarer's men should come to the toll-house along with the rest, and there renew their pledges and be enrolled on the town reeve's roll, and there pay him the penny called 'borthsilver',* of which the cellarer should have half. At the present time the cellarer receives nothing at all from that source. This was all done so that everyone should enjoy equal rights. The burgesses, however, still maintain that the suburban dwellers ought not to be free from toll in the market unless they are members of the guild-merchant. But now the reeve—the abbot turning a blind eye—claims for himself the pleas and forfeitures arising from the cellarer's fee.

The ancient customs of the cellarer, of which we have personal knowledge, were these. The cellarer had a messuage and barns near Scurun's well, where he was accustomed to hold his official court for robbers, and all pleas and suits. There he used to put his men in tithings, and enrol them, renewing this each year. He took the profits of the court in the same way that the reeve did at the borough court. This same messuage, with its adjacent garden (now held by the infirmarer), had been the manor-house of Beodric, lord of this town in ancient days, after whom the town used to be called 'Beodricsworth'. His fields are now in the demesne of the cellarer, and what is now called 'averland'* was the land of his peasants. The total estate that was held by him and his men consisted of 900 acres, and these lands are still the town fields. When the town was made free, the service owed for these lands was divided into two, in such a way that the sacrist or the reeve took a levy at the rate of 2d. per acre, and the cellarer had ploughing and other services, that is, from each acre was owed the service of ploughing one rood,* without food being provided for the ploughmen: this custom has been observed until now.

The cellarer also had sheep-folds where the townsmen, excepting the steward, who has his own fold, are bound to put their sheep: this custom has been observed until now. He also had 'averpeni'* at the rate of 2d. for every 30 acres: this custom was altered before the death of Abbot Hugh [1180], when Gilbert of Elveden was cellarer. The men of the town were accustomed, on the cellarer's orders, to go to Lakenheath and bring back eels from Southery [Norf.], as the carrying-service they owed. Often they would return empty-handed, and thus be put to trouble without bringing any benefit to the cellarer. So it was agreed between them and the cellarer that in future they should give 1d. a year for every 30 acres and stay at home. At the present time, however, those lands are divided into so many plots that it is scarcely known who ought to pay this tax. As a result, whereas in the past I have seen the cellarer take 27d. in one year, now he can hardly collect 10½d.

The cellarer also had the right to prevent anyone digging chalk or clay from the roads outside the town without his permission. In addition, he used to summon the fullers of the town to bring him cloths in which to carry his salt. If they did not comply he would prohibit them the use of the water, and take any cloths he could find.* These customs have been observed up to now.

Also, whoever bought grain or anything from the cellarer was free from toll at the town gate when he went out, for which reason the cellarer sold his goods at a higher price. This has been observed until now. Also, the cellarer is accustomed to take a toll on flax, at the time of retting,* at the rate of one bundle in each stook. Also, only the cellarer ought or is accustomed to have a free bull* in the fields of this town: now several people have them.

Also, when anyone made over a burgage tenement in free alms to the convent, and this was assigned to the cellarer or another obedientiary, that land used to be free from 'had-govel'* thereafter, most especially if it was assigned to the cellarer, on account of the dignity of his office, because he was second father in the monastery, or else on account of regard for the convent, because those who provide our food should be treated favourably. But the abbot says that this custom is unjust, because the sacrist loses out on his share.

Also, the cellarer used to guarantee the servants of the court that they should be free from scot and tallage.* But now it is not so, because the burgesses say that servants of the court ought to be free only in so far as they are servants, not because they hold burgage tenements in the town and they and their wives buy and sell in the market.

Also, the cellarer was accustomed to take freely, for his own uses, all dung in the streets of the town, except outside the doors of those who hold 'averland'. They alone were allowed to collect and keep the dung. This custom declined a little at the time of Abbot Hugh, until Denis and Roger of Ingham were made cellarers. They, wanting to revive the former custom, seized the burgesses' wagons laden with manure, and ordered them to be unloaded; but a great many burgesses protested, with such success that now each person collects the manure on his own tenement, and poor people sell theirs when and to whom they wish.

Also, the cellarer has a customary privilege in the town market, that he or his buyers for the convent shall have first pick of all the food, if the abbot is away from home. [If, however, the abbot is here,] whoever comes first to the market—the buyers for the abbot or those for the cellarer—shall purchase first, whether the one or the other. But if they arrive at the same moment, the abbot's buyers are to have priority. ⟨Also, when herrings are sold, the abbot's men always buy 100 herrings at a halfpenny less than the others; likewise the cellarer and his buyers. Also, if a quantity of fish or other food is delivered first to the court, or to the market, before it has been unloaded from horse or cart, the cellarer or his buyers may purchase it all and take it away free of toll.⟩* Abbot Samson, however, directed his buyers to give precedence to the cellarer and his men because, as he said, he would rather go short himself than have his convent do so. The buyers, therefore, 'in honour preferring one another' [Rom. 12: 10], if they find anything for sale which is not enough for both parties, buy it jointly and share it equally: and so, as between head and limbs, and between father and sons, 'A discordant harmony remains' [cf. Lucan 1. 98].

As the poet said, 'Envy aims at the highest' [Ovid, *Rem. Amor*. 369]. I quote this because when a certain person here looked at what I had written, and read of so many fine deeds, he accused me of flattering the abbot and seeking his grace and favour, saying that I had concealed certain things which should not be hushed up. And when I asked which and what sort of things, he answered, 'Don't you see that the abbot grants away escheats of lands which belong to the convent, and gives in marriage, as he pleases, young heiresses of lands and widows,* both in St Edmund's town and outside? Don't you see how the abbot takes for himself suits and pleas of those who claim by royal writ lands which are on the convent's fee, and most especially he hears those pleas that are profitable, leaving for the cellarer or the sacrist or other officials those pleas where a profit is not assured?' I replied to this for good or ill so far as I knew, saying that each feudal lord to whom homage was due ought to have the right of escheat when it occurs on a fee where he has received homage, and for the same reason all those things—a general aid from the burgesses, wardships of boys, and bestowals of widows and young women—seem to be appropriate to the abbot alone on those fees where he takes homage, except when the abbacy is vacant. In the town of St Edmund, however, the custom has evolved, because it is a borough, that the nearest relative should have wardship of the heir and his lands until he comes of age. Also concerning the suits and pleas, I replied that I had never seen the abbot usurp our pleas, unless we had failed to do justice, but that he had accepted money from time to time, when he had used his authority to intervene so that suits and pleas might be brought to their proper conclusion. I have also known pleas which belonged to us to be heard on occasion in the abbot's court because there was no one to claim them for the convent at the beginning of the suit.*

Fire at St Edmund's shrine 1198

IN 1198 the glorious martyr Edmund wanted to strike terror into our convent and instruct us that his body should be looked after more reverently and carefully. There was a wooden dais between the shrine and the high altar, on which there stood two candles which the wardens of the shrine used to patch up, piling wax on top of wax and crudely joining them. Under the dais many items had been put most inappropriately—flax, thread, wax, various implements, indeed anything that came into the hands of the wardens was stored there, the doors and walls being of iron. While the wardens slept on the night of St Etheldreda [22 June 1198],* it happened, so we believe, that part of a repaired candle burnt out on the said dais, which was covered with hangings, and began to ignite all about it, above and below, so that the iron walls glowed all over with fire. And 'Behold the wrath of the Lord' [Num. 11: 33], though not without mercy: as it is written, 'in wrath, thou wilt remember mercy' [Hab. 3: 2]. Around the same time the clock struck for Matins, and the vestry master, on getting up, saw the fire, and ran as fast as he could, and beat upon the board* as if someone were dead, and shouted in a loud voice that the shrine was on fire. We all rushed up, and met the incredibly fierce flames that were engulfing the whole shrine and almost reaching up to the beams of the church. Our young monks ran for water, some to the rain-water tank, some to the clock,* and some, with great difficulty, when they had snatched up the reliquaries, put out the flames with their hoods. When cold water was thrown on the front of the shrine, the precious stones fell down and were almost pulverized. Moreover, the nails by which the sheets of silver were held to the shrine came loose from the wood underneath, which was burnt to the thickness of my finger, and without the nails the sheets were hanging one from another. Yet the golden Majesty on the front of the shrine, with some of the stones, remained stable and intact, and was more beautiful after the fire than before, because it was solid gold.

It so happened, by God's will, that at that time the great beam which used to be beyond the altar had been taken down to be renovated with new carving. By chance, too, the cross and the 'Mariola' and the 'John', and the casket with the shirt of St Edmund, and the monstrances with the relics that used to hang from the same beam, and other reliquaries that stood on the beam*—all had been taken down earlier: otherwise everything would surely have been destroyed by the fire, as was the painted hanging which had been put up in place of the beam. But what would have been the outcome if the whole church had been decorated with hangings? Our despair was somewhat alleviated when, after careful investigation of the cracks and holes, we had made certain that the fire had not spread into the shrine at any point, and when we had established that everything had cooled down. Then, to our horror, some of our brethren shouted out with a loud wailing that St Edmund's cup was burnt. But when some of them were looking here and there among the cinders and ashes for stones and sheets of precious metal, they drew out the cup in perfect condition lying in a heap of cinders that were no longer burning, and they found it wrapped in a linen cloth that was half burnt. The oak box itself, in which the cup had long been stored, was burnt to dust, and only the iron bands and lock were found. When we saw this miracle, we all wept for joy.

Seeing that the greater part of the front of the shrine had lost its plating, and horrified by the shameful circumstances of the fire, we agreed together to summon a goldsmith secretly, and we made him join the metal sheets and re-affix them to the shrine as quickly as possible to avoid public disgrace. We had the scorch marks covered over with wax and other materials. But to quote the Evangelist, 'There is nothing covered that shall not be revealed' [Luke 12: 2]. The pilgrims who came early the next morning to make their offerings knew nothing of what had happened, but some of them, looking all around, asked where the fire was, which they had heard had occurred in the area of the shrine? Since it could not be entirely concealed, we replied to the questioners that a candle had fallen down and three towels had been burned, and that some stones in the front of the shrine had been destroyed by the heat of the flames. However, a flagrant lie was put about that the Saint's head had been burnt—some said only the hair, but later when they learned the truth, 'the mouth of them that speak lies was stopped' [Ps. 63: 11]. All this happened, by the will of God, so that the area round the shrine might be more carefully supervised and the abbot's plan carried out more speedily and without delay: this was to place the shrine, with the body of the holy martyr, more safely and more spectacularly in a higher position. Before this unfortunate accident the canopy of the shrine had been half completed and the marble blocks for raising and supporting the shrine had for the most part been prepared and polished.

The abbot, who was away, received the news with very great sorrow. On his return home, he came into chapter and said that all this had occurred—and similar, even greater disasters might come about—because of our sins, and especially because of our complaints about the food and drink. In saying this, he put the blame on the whole of the convent rather than on the wardens of the shrine for their greed and carelessness. In order to induce us to forgo our pittances for at least a year, and assign the pittancery funds to repairing the front of the shrine in solid gold, he himself first set an example of generosity and in front of us all contributed his entire gold treasure—fifteen gold rings, probably worth 60 marks—for the restoration of the shrine. We all agreed that our pittancery must be used for this purpose, but this decision was reversed because the sacrist said that St Edmund could well restore his own shrine without such help.

At that time a distinguished person—I don't know who—came and recounted to the abbot a vision he had had. The abbot was much moved, and narrated it in full chapter, adding some very severe comments. He said, 'What a man of importance has seen in a vision is true, namely that the holy martyr Edmund appeared to be lying outside his shrine, groaning, and seemed to say that he had been robbed of his clothes, and that he was emaciated from hunger and thirst, and that his burial-place and the portals of his church were badly cared for.' The abbot interpreted this dream to us all, laying the blame on us in this way: 'St Edmund states that he is naked because you deny the naked poor your old clothing, and it is with reluctance that you give what you ought to give; similarly with food and drink. The idleness of the sacrist and his officers—amounting to negligence—is obvious from the recent calamitous fire that broke out between the shrine and the altar.'

The convent was saddened by these words, and after chapter several brothers gathered together and explained the dream as follows: 'We', they said, 'are the naked limbs of St Edmund, and the convent is his naked body, because we have been robbed of our ancient customs and liberties. The abbot has everything—chamber, sacristy, cellary— and we are dying of hunger and thirst. We only get our

subsistence through the abbot's clerk and his administration. If the wardens of the shrine are negligent, let the
abbot blame himself, because he himself appointed them.'
Many in the convent spoke in this fashion. But when this
interpretation of the dream was revealed to the abbot, in
the forest of Harlow [Essex] as he was returning from
London, he was very angry and upset, and said in reply:
'Do they wish to use this dream against me? By God's
mouth, as soon as I get home I shall reinstate the customs
which they say belong to them, and I shall remove my clerk
from the cellary and let them get on with it: I will see their
good sense in a year's time. This year I stayed at home and
saved their cellary from debt, and this is how they show
their gratitude!' Returning home, and having in mind the
translation of the holy martyr, the abbot humbled himself
before God and man, resolving to turn over a new leaf and
restore good relations with everybody, most especially with
his convent. As he presided in chapter, therefore, he
ordered a cellarer and subcellarer to be elected by us all,
and he removed his clerk, saying that whatever he had done
had been to our advantage, to which God and His saints
bore witness, and he made numerous excuses.

The opening of St Edmund's tomb 1198

'HEAR, O heavens, and give ear, O earth!' [Isa. 1: 2] to
the achievement of Abbot Samson. With the Feast of St
Edmund approaching, the marble blocks were polished and
everything was ready for the elevation of the shrine. The
Feast was celebrated on a Friday [20 November 1198]. On
the following Sunday, a three-day fast was enjoined on the
people, and the reason for the fast was made known to
them publicly. The abbot warned the convent beforehand
that they should get ready to transfer the body on the
Monday night, and to move the shrine and set it on the
high altar until the masons' work was complete. And he

fixed the time for this operation and outlined the way in which it was to be done.

That night when we came to Matins, the great shrine stood empty on the high altar, prepared with a lining of white tawed deer skins, above, below, and round about, which were fixed to the wood by silver nails. One panel stood on the ground, against a column, and the Saint's body still lay where it had always been. When we had chanted Lauds, all went to receive the discipline.* That done, the abbot and those with him were vested in albs,* and approaching reverently, as was proper, they made haste to open the coffin. On the outside, covering the coffin and everything else, there was a linen cloth, which they found tied on top with cords. Underneath was a silk cloth, and then another linen cloth, and then a third, and so at last the coffin was uncovered, standing on a wooden tray so that it could not be damaged by the marble. A golden angel, the length of a man's foot, was attached to the outside of the coffin over the martyr's breast. The angel had a golden sword in one hand and a banner in the other, and immediately below there was an opening in the coffin-lid, through which, in the past, wardens of the shrine used to put their hands to touch the holy body. Written above the figure was the line: 'Behold, Michael's image guards the sacred corpse.' There were iron rings at the two ends of the coffin, like those usually found on a Norse chest. Lifting up the coffin with the body, they carried it to the altar, and as I helped to carry it, I placed my sinful hand on it, although the abbot had forbidden anyone to come forward unless summoned. So the coffin was enclosed in the shrine, and the panel was put back and refitted.

We all thought that the abbot intended to show the coffin to the people during the week after the Feast and to reinstate the Saint's body in the shrine in front of them all, but we were quite wrong, as will be clear from what follows. On the Wednesday [25 November], while the convent was singing Compline, the abbot discussed the matter with the sacrist and Walter the physician, and it was agreed that twelve brothers should be called who were strong enough to lift the panels of the shrine and skilled enough to take them apart and fit them together again. The abbot said that he longed to see his patron and that he wished to have the sacrist and Walter the physician with him at the inspection. Those chosen were the abbot's two chaplains, the two wardens of the shrine, the two vestry masters, and another six—Hugh the sacrist, Walter the physician, Augustine, William of Diss, Robert, and Richard. While the convent slept, these twelve were vested in albs, and lifting the coffin from the shrine, they carried it and placed it on a table near the old site of the shrine. They prepared to take off the lid, which was fixed to the coffin by sixteen very long nails. When they had completed this difficult task, they were all ordered to stand well back, except for the abbot's two companions mentioned above.

The coffin fitted the holy corpse so perfectly, both in length and in breadth, that a needle could scarcely have been inserted between the wood and either the head or the feet, and the head was joined to the body, a little raised on a small cushion. The abbot, then, looking closely, first came upon a silk cloth covering the whole body, and after that a linen cloth of wonderful whiteness, and over the head a small linen cloth, and then another fine-spun silk cloth, like the veil of a nun. And after that they found the corpse wrapped in linen, and then at last all the features of the Saint's body were visible.

At this point the abbot stopped, saying that he dare not proceed further and see the Saint's naked flesh. So taking the head in his hands, he groaned as he said, 'O glorious martyr St Edmund, blessed be the hour in which you were born. O glorious martyr, do not cast me, a miserable sinner, into perdition for daring to touch you; you understand my devotion and purpose.' And he proceeded to touch the eyes and the very large and prominent nose, and then he felt the breast and the arms, and raising the left hand, he took hold of the Saint's fingers and put his fingers between them. Continuing, he found that the feet were stiffly upright, as of a man who had died that very day, and he felt the toes, counting them as he went. Then it was decided that some other brothers should be called to witness these marvels, and six were summoned and came, and with them six more appeared without the abbot's permission, and viewed the Saint's body—they were Walter of St Albans, Hugh the infirmarer, Gilbert the prior's brother, Richard of Ingham, Jocellus the cellarer, and Thurstan the Little, who was the only one to put his hand on the feet and knees of the Saint. And so that there should be plenty of witnesses, by the will of the Almighty, one of our brothers, John of Diss, who was perching in the vault with the vestry servants, saw everything plainly.

Next, the martyr was wrapped in the same cloths and in the same order, just as he had been found, and then the lid was put back on the coffin using the same sixteen nails in the same way. And then the coffin was returned to its usual position, and there was placed on the coffin, next to the angel, a silk box, in which was deposited a parchment document written in English, which contained, I think, some salutations of the monk Ailwin.* This document had been found beside the golden angel when the coffin was uncovered. On the abbot's orders another document was now written and stowed away in the box. This is what it said: 'In 1198 on the night after the Feast of St Katherine [25 November],* Abbot Samson, out of devotion, saw and touched the body of St Edmund. There were present . . .' and there followed the names of the eighteen monks. The brothers now wrapped the whole coffin in a suitable linen cloth, and placed on the top a precious new silk cloth, which Archbishop Hubert of Canterbury had given them that year, and next to the stone surrounds they put a linen cloth, doubled to the length of the coffin, so that neither the coffin nor its tray should be damaged by the stone. Then the panels were brought and carefully joined to the shrine. When the convent gathered for Matins and saw this, all those who had not been present were sad, saying among themselves, 'We have been badly misled.' But when Matins was over, the abbot summoned the convent to the high altar, and briefly showing them what had been done, he explained that it was neither right nor practicable for everyone to have been called to witness these things. After we had listened to him, we tearfully sang the 'Te Deum', and made haste to ring the bells in choir.

Three days later [28 November] the abbot dismissed the wardens of the shrine and the warden of St Botulph's shrine; he appointed new wardens and drew up regulations for the better and more diligent care of the sanctuaries. He had the high altar, which had previously been hollow, and where items had frequently been put away in an inappropriate manner, and also the space between the shrine and the altar, filled in with stone and cement, so that there should be no danger of fire through the wardens' negligence, as there had been before. According to the wise man's dictum, 'Happy is he who learns from the mishaps of others.'

King John visits—abbot and monks quarrel 1199

WHEN the abbot had bought the grace and favour of King Richard with gifts and money, and accordingly believed that he would be able to bring all his plans to a successful conclusion, King Richard died [6 April 1199], and the abbot's labour and expense were wasted. But King John, ignoring all his other commitments, came to St Edmund's immediately after his coronation, impelled by a vow and out of devotion. We naturally thought that he would make a sizeable donation, but he gave only a silk cloth which his servants had on loan from our sacrist—and still they have not paid for it. Although he had accepted St Edmund's most generous hospitality, when he left he contributed nothing at all honourable or beneficial to the Saint, except the 13s. which he gave at Mass on the day he left us.

At this time some of our obedientiaries alleged in chapter that our serjeant Ralph the gatekeeper* was pursuing certain cases and lawsuits against them, to the detriment of the church and to the disadvantage of the convent. With everyone's agreement, the prior ordered that he should be punished in the customary manner for servants, that is by the loss of his wages. The cellarer was instructed, therefore, to withdraw not the corrody* that belonged to the gatekeeper's office as granted in his terms of employment, but certain additional payments and allowances which the cellarer and the subcellarer had given him without asking the convent. When the abbot returned from London, however, this same Ralph, accompanied by some of the abbot's servants, complained to the abbot that the prior and convent had robbed him of the corrody which he had possessed when the abbot was first elected. They also informed the abbot that this had been done in his absence, to his dishonour and arbitrarily, because he had not been consulted and no reason was given. The abbot believed them, and was uncharacteristically agitated, and more than the matter warranted. He unwaveringly excused Ralph and declared him innocent, and coming into chapter he complained that this action had been taken to his disadvantage and without his being consulted. Someone replied, and everybody else shouted in agreement, that it had been done by the prior with the unanimous approval of the chapter. The abbot was disconcerted by this, and said, '"I have nourished and brought up children, and they have rejected me" [Isa. 1: 2]'. Instead of overlooking the affair, which would have been the proper way to maintain harmonious relations, and not wanting to admit that he had been defeated, he demonstrated his power by publicly commanding the cellarer to restore in full everything that had been taken from Ralph. Nor was the cellarer to have anything to drink but water until full restitution had been made. When Jocellus the cellarer heard this he chose to drink water for the day rather than restore Ralph's corrody against the convent's decision. On the next day, when the abbot learned of this, he prohibited the cellarer both food and drink until everything was given back, and he left the town immediately after issuing this edict and stayed away for a week. On the day the abbot went, the cellarer got up in chapter, and brandishing the abbot's written command, and holding his keys in his hand, he announced that he would rather be deposed from his office than do anything in opposition to the convent.

Then there was a great uproar in the convent, such as I have never seen before, and it was said that the abbot's command should not be obeyed. The older and wiser members of the convent, however, tactfully kept silent, eventually declaring that the abbot must be obeyed in all things unless clearly contrary to God's will, and they were agreed that for the time being we should suffer this disgrace for the sake of peace, lest relations should deteriorate further. But when the prior began to chant 'Ponder my words, O Lord' [Ps. 5], from the Office for the Dead, as was customary,* the novices, and with them almost half the convent, protested and objected at the top of their voices. However, the senior members prevailed, although they were in the minority compared with the rest who were numerous.

Then the abbot, who was not present but acting through intermediaries, frightened some by threats, won over others by flattery, and isolated from the rest of the community the more important men of the convent (who seemed to be afraid of his very cassock), so that the words of the gospel were fulfilled, 'Every kingdom divided against itself shall be brought to desolation' [Matt. 12: 25]. And the abbot declared that he would not associate with us at all, because of the plots and sworn agreements which he alleged we had made to stab him to death with our knives.

So when he came home, he stayed in his lodgings, and summoned one of our brothers, of whom he was most suspicious, to come to see him. And when he did not come, for fear of being imprisoned and put in chains, he was excommunicated, and later he was shackled for a whole day and stayed in the infirmary until morning. The abbot passed a lighter sentence on three others to intimidate the rest. On the next day it was decided that the abbot should be sent for and that we should submit to him in word and demeanour, to placate him. And so this was done. In fact he replied quite humbly, yet always maintaining his position and turning the blame on us; when he saw that we accepted defeat, he too was overcome. With tears streaming down, he swore that he had never lamented so much as this over anything, both for himself and for us, and most especially because of the stain of an evil report that had already made our dissension publicly known, to the effect that the monks of St Edmund's wanted to murder their abbot. And when the abbot had told how he had deliberately kept away until his anger had cooled, quoting the philosopher's saying, 'I would have revenged myself on you had I not been angry', he stood up weeping, and embraced everyone with the kiss of peace. He wept: we wept too. The brothers who had been excommunicated were absolved on the spot, and so 'the storm ceased and there was a great calm' [Mark 4: 39]. The abbot, however, secretly ordered that the usual corrody should be fully restored to Ralph the gatekeeper as before; we turned a blind eye when we at last comprehended that there is no lord who does not wish to domineer, and that a struggle is dangerous when it is started and waged against a stronger and more powerful adversary.

The survey of knights' fees 1200

IN the year 1200 a survey was made of the knights of St Edmund and of their fees, in which their predecessors had been enfeoffed:*

Aubrey de Vere has five and a half knights' fees, i.e. in Loddon and Broome [both Norf.] one fee; in Mendham and Preston one fee; in Rede one fee; in Cockfield a half fee; and in Livermere two fees.

William de Hastings has five fees, i.e. in Lidgate, Blunham [Beds.], and [West] Harling [Norf.] three fees; and in Tibenham and Gissing [both Norf.] two fees.

Earl Roger [Bigod] has three fees in Norton and Bressingham [Norf.].

Robert son of Roger has one fee in Marlesford.

Alexander of Kirby has one fee in Kirby [Kirby Cane, Norf.].

Roger de Hou has two fees in Mickfield and Topcroft [Norf.].

Arnold de Charneles and his parceners* have one fee in Oakley, Quidenham [Norf.], Thurston, and Stuston.

Osbert of Waxham [Norf.] has one fee in Marlingford [Norf.] and Wortham.

William of Tostock has one fee in Thrandeston.

Gilbert son of Ralph has three fees, i.e. in Thelnetham and Hepworth one fee; in Reydon and Gissing [Norf.] one fee; and in Saxham one fee.

Ralph of Buckenham has a half fee in Old Buckenham [Norf.].

William of Bardwell has two fees in Barningham, Bardwell, Hunston, and Stanton.

Robert de Langtoft has three fees in Stow [Stowlangtoft], Ashfield, Troston, and Little Waltham in Essex.

Adam of Cockfield has two fees, i.e. in Lavenham and Onehouse one fee; and in Lindsey [one fee].

Robert son of Walter has one fee in Fakenham Magna and Sapiston.

William Blund has one fee in [Ixworth] Thorpe.

Gilbert Pecche has two fees, i.e. in 'Waude' and Gedding one fee; and in Felsham, Euston, and Groton one fee.

Gilbert of St Clare has two fees in Bradfield [Bradfield St Clare] and Wattisfield.

Geoffrey of Welnetham and Gilbert of Manston have one fee in Welnetham and Manston.

Hubert de Anesty has a half fee in Briddinghoe [Bennington Hall, in Witham, Essex].

Gervase de Roinghe has one fee in 'Clipeleie' [?Chipley] and 'Roinghe' [?Roding, Essex].

Robert of Hawstead has one fee in Hawstead and a half fee in Brockley.

Reginald of Brockley has one fee in Brockley.

Simon of Pattishall has a half fee in Whatfield.

Peter son of Alan has a half fee in Brockley.

Ralph de Presseni has a half fee in Stanningfield.

Richard of Ickworth has two fees in Ickworth and Wangford.

Robert of Horningsheath has a half fee in Horningsheath.

Walter of Saxham has one fee in Ashfield and Saxham.

William of Wordwell has half a fee in Welnetham.

Norman of Risby has a half fee in Risby.

Peter of Livermere and Alan of Flempton have one fee in Livermere and Ampton.

Roger de Morieux has one fee in Thorpe [Thorpe Morieux].

Hugh of Eleigh has two fees in [?Brent] Eleigh, Preston, and Bradfield.

Stephen of Brockdish has a quarter fee in Brockdish [Norf.].

Adam of Barningham has a quarter fee in Barningham.
William of Wordwell has a quarter fee in Little Livermere
and Wordwell.

Four conventual manors—the
Cockfield dispute

OUR monk Geoffrey Rufus, although he behaved in too
worldly a style, was of assistance to us in looking after four
manors—Barton [Great Barton], Pakenham, Rougham,
and Bradfield [Bradfield Combust]—where formerly we
had often been short on the rents.* The abbot heard
rumours of his misconduct, but ignored them for a long
time, perhaps because Geoffrey seemed to be of service to
everybody. But eventually, when he realized the whole
truth, he had his coffers seized at once and placed in the
vestry, and all the stock of the manors carefully guarded,
and he had Geoffrey himself confined to the monastery. A
large amount of gold and silver was found, 200 marks in
value, all of which the abbot said should be put towards
constructing the front of St Edmund's shrine. With
Michaelmas approaching [29 September], it was decided in
chapter that two brothers, not just one alone, should take
charge of the manors. One was Roger of Ingham, who gave
a public assurance that he was willing and could easily look
after both the manors and the cellary. The abbot consented
to this, although the convent was unwilling: and Jocellus,
who had ably and providently carried out his duties, and,
unlike other cellarers, had run the cellary without debt for
two years, was dismissed and made subcellarer. At the end
of the year, however, when Roger the cellarer accounted
for his receipts and expenditure, he acknowledged that he
had taken 60 marks from the stock of the manors to make
good the losses on the cellary. When some discussion had
taken place, therefore, the said Jocellus was restored to the

cellary and was given the manors of Mildenhall, Chepenhall, and Southwold. The other manors were put in the charge of Roger and Albinus, and were separated from the cellary, so that the manors should not be weakened by the cellary, nor the cellary by the manors.

On Adam of Cockfield's death [?1198], the abbot could have taken 300 marks for the wardship of Adam's only daughter, but because her grandfather had secretly taken her away, the abbot was not able to get hold of the girl without the help of Archbishop Hubert of Canterbury, so he granted her wardship to the archbishop for the sum of £100.* The archbishop sold her wardship for 500 marks to Thomas de Burgh, brother of [Hubert de Burgh] the king's chamberlain,* and the girl, with all her rights, was given to him with the abbot's consent. Thomas therefore at once sought possession of the three manors—Cockfield, Semer, and Groton—which were in our hands after Adam's death. But we were of the opinion that we could keep them all in our demesne, or at least two of them—Semer and Groton: firstly because Robert of Cockfield, nearing his end, had said in front of witnesses that he could not claim those two manors by hereditary right, and secondly because his son Adam, in open court, had resigned those two manors to us and had made a charter to this effect, in which it was stated that he held those two manors as a favour from the convent for his lifetime only.* Thomas, therefore, seeking to get a writ of recognition on this, had knights summoned to go to Tewkesbury to appear on oath before the king [April 1201].* Our charter cut no ice when read in public because the whole court was against us. The knights said on oath that they knew nothing of our charters or of any private agreements, but believed Adam and his father and his grandfather had held the manors for the past hundred years in fee farm, one following another without any break in the succession. And so, after much trouble and expense, we were dispossessed by a court judgement, and retained only the ancient annual rents.

The abbot appeared to have been deluded by the outward forms of rectitude, as the Scripture says, 'I will not give my glory unto another' [Isa. 42: 8; 48: 1], because when the abbot of Cluny came here [1201], and we had respectfully received him, our abbot would not give precedence to him, either in chapter or in the Sunday procession, but sat and stood between him and [Bertrand] abbot of Chertsey.* This prompted much varied comment.

A new prior chosen 1201

WHEN Robert the prior lay very weak and close to death,* there were many opinions about who should succeed him as prior. Somebody reported that the abbot, sitting in choir and considering all the brethren one by one, did not find anyone whom he felt called upon to make prior except his chaplain, Herbert. The abbot's choice became clear to many from this and other similar reports. There was one man who, on hearing of it, said that it was incredible: he maintained that the abbot, a diligent and wise man, 'will never give the prior's office to such a person as this'— young, almost beardless, a novice for twelve years, and a cloister monk for only four, who had no experience of spiritual counselling or knowledge of doctrine.

When the prior died, the abbot was staying in London. Somebody commented, 'It is not yet a month since the abbot made Herbert, his chaplain, subsacrist, and when he conferred that office on him in the chapel of St Nicaise he promised him he would make him prior if he could, and would do all in his power to bring this about.' On hearing this, someone who wished to please both the abbot and the future prior canvassed many monks—seniors and juniors alike—that when the opportunity arose they should put forward Herbert's name for the priorate, or at the very least include his along with other names. He swore that in this way they would please the abbot because Herbert was the abbot's choice. Indeed, there were many, both seniors and juniors, who found Herbert an amiable and affable man and worthy of high office.

On the other hand, there were others, few in number, it is true, but the more respected and experienced section of the convent, who wanted Master Hermer the subprior to be promoted to the priorate—a man of maturity, literate and eloquent, skilled and experienced in spiritual counselling, who at that time had presided over cloister discipline for fourteen years, and had proved himself a dedicated subprior. This man, I say, was the one they wished to promote as prior, according to the wise saying, 'Trust the experienced master' [Virgil, *Aeneid*, xi. 283]. The majority, however, snorted their opposition, describing him as an irascible man, impatient, restless, boisterous and troublesome, litigious and quarrelsome, and they ridiculed him, quoting, 'The discretion of a man deferreth his anger' [Prov. 19: 11]. But one brother spoke as follows: 'It would prove a tremendous and fearful scandal should the subprior be set aside: educated clerks would in future disdain to take the habit here if it turns out that ours is the kind of convent where a speechless figurehead is set up and a block of wood promoted.' And he added that the prior of our convent ought to be a person of such standing that, should any important ecclesiastical or secular matter arise when the abbot was away, it could be referred to him as a man of substance and discretion. Another brother, hearing this and similar comments, said, 'Why do you keep talking like this? When the abbot comes home he will do exactly as he pleases: perhaps he will make a great show of consulting a few of us individually, but ultimately, using persuasive and reasonable arguments, and in a roundabout manner, he will come down in favour of his own inclination, and the outcome will be what he has already decided.'

After the abbot had returned, and was seated in chapter, he outlined in detail and with some eloquence what qualities the new prior ought to possess, to which John the third prior replied in front of everyone that the subprior was worthy and suitable. But immediately a large number exclaimed, 'A man of peace, give us a man of peace'. Two of us answered the majority that a man who knew how to give spiritual counsel and to distinguish 'between leprosy and leprosy' [Deut. 17: 8] ought to be appointed, a comment that greatly displeased them as it seemed to favour the subprior's party. Then the abbot, observing the furore, said that he wished to hear the opinions of individual monks after chapter, so that he might proceed in an informed manner, and on the next day he would announce his decision. In the interim someone commented that the abbot had put on this show so that the subprior could be cleverly set aside as a candidate for the priorate, apparently on the advice of the convent and not on the abbot's direction. By this manoeuvre the abbot himself would be blameless, and 'the mouth of them that speak lies might be stopped' [Ps. 63: 11].

On the following day, when the abbot was seated in chapter, he announced with many tears that he had spent a sleepless night through worry and fear that he might nominate someone displeasing to God. And he swore on peril of his soul that he would choose four from amongst our number who in his opinion were the most worthy and suitable, for us to elect one of them. The abbot nominated first of all the sacrist—who was known to be weak and incompetent, as the man himself immediately declared, with an oath, in front of us all. Then the abbot nominated his relative, John the third prior, Maurice, his chaplain, and Herbert, mentioned above: all these were young men aged 40 or less, with a smattering of education, and though receptive, they were not qualified, but rather required instruction in spiritual counselling. The abbot put these three on his short list, placing them above the subprior and several other senior monks, who were important, mature, and learned, including former schoolmasters, not to mention everybody else. The abbot spent a long time describing and praising many aspects of John's character, but against him he maintained that if he was made prior his many relatives in this area would be a weight around his neck. The abbot intended to say something similar about Maurice, as well he might, contriving finally to come to Herbert, when suddenly he was interrupted by one of the more important brothers, who said, 'Dom Precentor, you have the right to speak first: nominate Dom Herbert.' To which the precentor replied, 'He is a good man.' When the abbot heard the name of Herbert, he halted in what he had to say, and turning to the precentor he said, 'I will accept Herbert with pleasure if it is your wish.' At these words, the whole convent shouted, 'He is a good man, a good man, and worthy of affection', and a number of the more prominent monks agreed with this. Immediately the precentor and one of his colleagues, and two from the other side, rose hurriedly and caused Herbert to stand in the middle. But at first Herbert humbly declined. He said that he was not fit for such an office, most especially because, as he declared, he had not enough learning to know how to preach a sermon in chapter that would be worthy of a prior. Many of us who witnessed these events were stupefied and struck dumb with amazement. The abbot, however, to comfort him, and speaking as if to belittle men of learning, replied lengthily that he could quite well memorize and re-use other people's sermons, as was not unusual. And he went on to condemn colourful rhetoric and flowery words and exquisite prose in sermons, maintaining that in many churches the sermon is given to the convent in French, or more appropriately in English, so as to be edifying rather than showily learned. At these words, the new prior went up to the abbot and kissed his feet. The abbot received him tearfully, and led him by the hand to the prior's stall, and commanded everybody to show him the reverence and obedience due to the prior.

When the chapter meeting finished, I, the guest-master, sat in the lobby of the guest-house hall, dumbfounded, turning over in my mind what I had seen and heard. I began to think carefully why, and for what qualities, such a man should be promoted to such a high office. And I came to realize that he was a man of good build and handsome personal appearance, with a beautiful face and an amiable expression, always cheerful, who smiled all day long, benevolent to everyone. He was restrained in gesture, dignified in movement, polished in speech, with a melodious singing voice and a fine reading voice; young, strong, and physically healthy, and ready to work for the good of the church. He knew well how to adapt himself—according to the demands of time and place—to laymen and clerks, to ecclesiastics and men of the world. Liberal, sociable, and easy in manner; not eager to find fault; not suspicious or avaricious; neither over-zealous nor lazy; sober; fluent in everyday French, being a Norman; a man of average intelligence, who, 'if learning were to make him mad' [Acts 26: 24], might be called a man of perfect accomplishment. When I pondered on these points I said to myself that the man was popular, but that 'nothing is entirely perfect' [Horace, *Odes*, II. xvi. 27–8], and crying for joy I said, '"That God hath visited" us [Luke 7: 6]; "as it hath pleased the Lord, so hath it been done" [Job 1: 21].' But suddenly another thought came to me—'Spare your praises of the new man, because high office changes a man's character, or rather demonstrates its true nature. First take note of which advisers he has, and what they are like, and in whom he trusts, because like naturally attracts like. "The outcome will be the test of what is done" [Ovid, *Heroides*, ii. 85], and so spare your praises.'

That same day some of the uneducated brothers, both

obedientiaries and cloister monks, came together and
secretly sharpened their tongues 'to shoot out their arrows'
[Ps. 64: 3–4] at the educated. Recalling the abbot's
remarks, made that very day in apparent disparagement of
men of learning, they said to one another, 'Now let our
philosophers understand the consequences of their philoso-
phizing! Now it is clear what comes of their philosophy!
Our good clerks have done so much declining in the cloister
that they have all been declined! There has been so much
sermonizing in chapter that they are all rebuffed! They
have talked so much about distinguishing "between leprosy
and leprosy" [Deut. 17: 8] that they have been thrown out
as lepers themselves! They have declined *musa, muse* so
often that their minds are reckoned to be muzzy!' They
made these and similar comments to deride and pour scorn
on others, and being aware of their own ignorance they
condemned learning and belittled educated men. They were
full of rejoicing and high hopes, which will never perhaps
come to fruition, since 'fair hope is often deceived in its
own promise' [Ovid, *Heroides*, xvii. 234].

Samson's faults

As the wise man said, no one 'is entirely perfect' [Horace,
Odes, II. xvi. 27–8]—and neither was Abbot Samson. I
would say this because, in my judgement, the abbot is not
to be praised for having ordered a charter to be drawn up
giving the serjeanty of John Rufus to one of his own
servants after John's death: it was said that 10 marks
'blinded the eyes of the wise' [Deut. 16: 19]. When our
monk Denis told him that such an action was unheard of,
the abbot answered, 'I will not be deflected from carrying
out my intention for your sake any more than I would for
that young whipper-snapper there.' The abbot did the same
with the serjeanty of Adam of the infirmary, in return for

100s. It can be said of an action of that kind, that 'a little leaven leaveneth the whole lump' [1 Cor. 5: 6].

There is another stain of evil-doing which the abbot will wash away with the tears of contrition, if God wills, so that a single bad deed may not mar all the good. He has so raised the level of the fish-pond at Babwell, for the new mill, that there is not one man, rich or poor, who has land next to the river between the town gate and the east gate, who has not lost his garden and orchards as a result of the flooding. The cellarer's pasture, on the other bank, has been ruined, and the neighbours' arable land is spoiled. The cellarer's meadow has been destroyed, the infirmarer's orchard is submerged, and all the neighbours complain about it. But when the cellarer tackled him in chapter about the damage, the abbot replied, with a flash of anger, that he was not going to sacrifice his fish-pond for the sake of our meadow.

The dean of London writes in his chronicle as follows:*

King Henry II, having discussed the matter of vacant abbeys with the archbishop and bishops, observed the letter of the canon law on the appointment of abbots, using candidates begged from elsewhere. He considered perhaps that if pastors were chosen from their own flocks in all instances, earlier friendship might guarantee that offences would go unpunished, easy familiarity might encourage indulgence towards faults, and excessive lenience might pervade the cloisters.

Another has said:*

It seems better that a pastor should be chosen not from his own house, but rather from another. If he is promoted from elsewhere he will always believe, according to the size of the convent whose rule he has taken over, that there are many hard-working monks whose advice he should seek if he is a good man, but whose upright character he should be apprehensive of if he is bad. On the other hand, if he comes from the same house, he will be more aware of the inexperience, weakness, and inadequacy of each individual, and so will rage fearlessly, ramming 'a square peg into a round hole'.

For this reason the monks of Ramsey, when they were free to elect one of their own number, had they so wished, twice within living memory elected an abbot from another house.*

The monks of Ely and their market

IN 1201 the abbot of Flay* came to visit us. Through his preaching, and with the consent of the abbot, he ordered the public buying and selling which used to take place in the market on Sundays to be transferred to Tuesdays. He did likewise in other cities and boroughs throughout England.

In the same year the monks of Ely opened a market at Lakenheath: they had permission for this by royal charter. At first we dealt gently with them, as with friends and neighbours. We sent messengers to the Ely chapter, and letters and petitions in the first instance to the bishop of Ely, asking that they should stop this enterprise. We added that we would willingly pay them—for the sake of peace and the maintenance of good mutual relations between us—the 15 marks which they had given to get the king's charter. What more can I say? They would not desist, threats were exchanged, and 'spears were set against spears' [Lucan I. 7]. We acquired a writ of recognition as to whether a market, which was to our prejudice and to the disadvantage of St Edmund's market, should be held there. On oath it was stated that it was to our disadvantage. When the king was told of this, he ordered a search to be made through his register* as to precisely what charter he had given to the monks of Ely, and it was revealed that he had granted them the market on condition that it should not damage neighbouring markets. Then the king, on the promise of a mere

40 marks, gave us a charter that in future no market was to be held within St Edmund's Liberty without the abbot's consent. He wrote also to Geoffrey Fitz Peter, the justiciar,* that the market at Lakenheath should be discontinued. The justiciar wrote this to the sheriff of Suffolk, and the sheriff, knowing that he could not enter the Liberty of St Edmund or exercise any power there, ordered the abbot by writ to implement the king's command.

The bailiff of the hundred, therefore, went there [Lakenheath] on market-day, with freemen as witnesses, and on the king's behalf publicly prohibited that market, showing the letters from the king and the sheriff, but being treated to insults and injuries he withdrew without completing the business. The abbot put off the matter for a time, as he was in London. Then, taking wise advice, he ordered his bailiffs to gather together the men of St Edmund, with their horses and arms, and destroy the market, binding and bringing back with them any persons found buying and selling. And so in the middle of the night almost six hundred well-armed men set off for Lakenheath. But informants gave warning of their coming, so that everyone who was in the market scattered hither and thither, and not one was to be found. Suspecting the arrival of our men, the prior of Ely also came with his bailiffs on the same night to protect the buyers and sellers as best he could; but he would not come out of his house, and when our bailiffs sought securities from him, to stand trial in St Edmund's court concerning the said injury, he refused. So when the bailiffs had taken advice, they threw down the poles of the meat-market and the tables of the market stalls, and carried them away, and taking with them all the cattle, 'all sheep and oxen: yea and the beasts of the field' [Ps. 8: 7], they headed off for Icklingham. The prior's bailiffs followed, and asked to have their cattle for fifteen days in return for pledges, and this request was allowed. Within the fifteen days, the abbot was summoned by writ to come to the Exchequer to reply on this matter, and in the meantime to surrender the cattle. For the bishop of Ely [Eustace, 1198–1215], an eloquent and fluent speaker, had complained personally to the justiciar and magnates of England, that an act of unheard-of arrogance had taken place on St Etheldreda's land* in time of peace, for which reason many were enraged against the abbot.

Another dispute with Ely— Samson's leave-taking

MEANWHILE another disagreement arose between the bishop of Ely and the abbot. When a certain young man from Glemsford had been accused in St Edmund's court of a breach of the king's peace, and had been sought for a long time, both here and in the county, the bishop's steward at last produced the young man and claimed that he should be tried in St Etheldreda's court, on the basis of charters and privileges that he exhibited. Our bailiffs, seeking the suit and the general right [of jurisdiction], could not make themselves heard. The county court adjourned the case for the attention of the itinerant justices, and so St Edmund was dispossessed. When the abbot heard this he was proposing to go abroad,* but, because he was unwell, he deferred the matter until the Feast of the Purification [2 February 1202].

Then suddenly, on St Agnes' Day [21 January], a messenger came from the king, bringing a papal mandate which ordered the bishop of Ely and the abbot of St Edmund's to investigate the cases of Geoffrey Fitz Peter, William de Stuteville, and certain other magnates, who had taken the Cross.* The king had sought absolution for them, claiming that they were physically unfit and that he needed their counsel in the government of his kingdom. The messenger also brought a letter from the king, with the command that when the abbot had seen the letter, he should come and speak with the king about the pope's mandate. The abbot was agitated, and said: '"I am beset with trouble on every side" [Dan. 13: 22]: either I shall offend God or I shall offend the king. By the true God, whatever happens, I will not knowingly tell a lie.'

He hurried home, somewhat hampered by his physical infirmity, and through the prior he humbly, and with unaccustomed timidity, asked our advice—which he had rarely done before—as to how he should act to defend the liberties of the church; where the expenses should come from if he undertook this journey; to whom he should entrust the custody of the abbey; and what he should do about his poor servants who had been a long time in his service. The reply was that he should go in person, and that he should borrow sufficient money, to be repaid out of our sacristy, our pittances fund, and from our other resources, as he wished. He should hand over the care of the abbey to the prior and to a certain clerk, whom he had made rich, and who in the meantime would have to support himself, so saving the abbot the expense. To each of his servants he should give a sum of money assessed according to their previous service. He was grateful for this advice, and it was done as suggested. When the abbot came into chapter on the day before he was to leave, he had all his books brought in with him, and presented them to the church and convent; and he praised our good advice, which the prior had passed on to him.

Meanwhile we heard some people grumbling that whereas the abbot was diligent and careful for the liberties of his Barony, he had nothing to say about the liberties of the convent which we had lost during his rule—that is the liberties of the court and of the cellarer—nor about the rights of the sacrist over the convent's appointment of the town reeves. And so the Lord aroused the spirit of three monks of moderate intelligence who, when they had enlisted a number of others, went to ask the prior whether he would speak to the abbot and request on our behalf that before he left he should provide for his church's security in those liberties. On hearing this, the abbot said several things that should not have been said, and swore that he would be master as long as he lived. But with evening approaching, he spoke more mildly with the prior. Then on the next day, as he was about to leave, he said as he sat in chapter that he had settled all his servants peacefully and had made his will, as if he were about to die; and beginning to speak about the liberties, he gave as his excuse for changing the ancient customs that it was to avoid any failure of royal justice; and he put the blame on the sacrist, and said that if Durand, the town reeve, who was then ill, should die, the sacrist should take over the management of the reeve's office and should propose a reeve to the chapter, as was the ancient custom, although it must be done on the abbot's advice; but the gifts and yearly renders which were made by the reeve he would certainly not remit. When we enquired what was to be done about the loss of the cellarer's court, and especially about the halfpennies which the cellarer used to receive from the renewal of pledges, he was moved to question on what authority we should exercise a royal right and associated royal customs. The reply was that we have always had that right from the foundation of the church, and even during the first three years of his abbacy, and that we enjoy this right of the renewal of pledges in all our manors. We said that we ought not to lose our right for the sake of 100s., which he used to receive privately from the reeve each year, and we boldly petitioned for possession of the same rights as we had at the beginning of his abbacy. The abbot, as if put on the spot as to what he should reply, and wanting to leave us peacefully and go away on a harmonious note, ordered that those halfpennies, and other moneys which were the cellarer's, should be put in safe-keeping until he came home again. He also promised that on his return he would administer everything with our advice, arrange matters justly, and restore to each man what was his due. After this discussion there was calm, but not a great calm, because 'in promises anyone may be rich' [Ovid, *Ars Amat*. i. 444].

Appendix on the Cockfield tenancy by William of Diss*

ROBERT of Cockfield [in 1188] made a public recognition to Abbot Samson before a large number of people—Master W. of Banham [Norf.] and brother W[illiam] of Diss [Norf.], chaplains, William de Breitona and many others—that he had no hereditary right to the villages of Groton and Semer, for during the unsettled years of King Stephen's reign [probably the 1140s], the monks of St Edmund's, with the consent of their abbot, had conceded the two villages to his father, Adam of Cockfield, for a life term: in return for 100*s*. per annum for Semer and an annual food-rent for Groton. Adam was able to defend the manors against neighbouring castellans, W. of Milden and W. de Ambli, because he had a castle close by, at Lindsey.

After Adam's death [?mid-1150s], the monks granted these manors to his son Robert of Cockfield, doubling the yearly rent for Semer to £10, for as long as the abbot and convent wished. But he never, in the whole of his life, had a charter to this effect. For all the lands which he held from St Edmund by hereditary right, he had valid charters, which I, William of Diss, at that time chaplain, read in a public gathering in the presence of Abbot Samson. There was one for the lands of Lindsey, which Wulfric of Lindsey held in the town of St Edmund. He also had a charter of the abbot and convent concerning the rented tenancies of Rougham, which lady Rohais of Cockfield, wife of the late Adam II, has as her dowry. And he had another charter for the lands which his ancestor Lemmer* had held in the town of Cockfield by hereditary right and which were originally held from St Edmund as rented tenancies: in King Stephen's reign, with the assent of Abbot Anselm of St Edmund's [before 1148], these lands were assessed at half a knight's fee. Also he had charters from the abbot and convent for lands in the town of St Edmund. For the land of Humphrey Criketot, where the houses of the lady Alice were once situated, which is held for 12d. a year, the family has a charter and hereditary right. The large messuage, where the manor-house of Adam I of Cockfield formerly stood, with its wooden belfry 140 feet high, was confirmed to them in heredity for 2s. annually, by a charter of the abbot and convent: the length and breadth of the site and the messuage are defined in this charter. They also have hereditary right, by charter, to the lands which Robert of Cockfield, son of Odo of Cockfield, at present holds in Barton. But they have no charter for the village of Cockfield, that is to say the part which provides food for the monks of St Edmund's, other than a writ of King Henry I ordering Abbot Anselm to allow Adam I of Cockfield to hold undisturbed the farm of Cockfield, and others, as long as the food-rents are fully paid. This writ, however, has a seal impressed with a representation of the king on one side only, contrary to the accepted form of all royal writs. Robert of Cockfield, however, declared in the presence of the abbot and of the others named above that he believed Cockfield to be his by hereditary right on account of his long tenure, because his grandfather Lemmer had held the manor long before his death, and Lemmer's son, Adam I, held it during his lifetime, and Robert himself held it for his whole life, for almost sixty years, but they never had a charter from the abbot and convent of St Edmund's for this land.

EXPLANATORY NOTES

3 *the Flemings . . . outside the town*: a force of Flemish mercenaries, under Robert de Beaumont, earl of Leicester, landed at Walton (Felixstowe) in Suffolk, in support of Henry the young king's rebellion against his father, Henry II. They were defeated in autumn 1173 at Fornham St Genevieve on the River Lark, 4¼ miles from Bury.

Abbot Hugh . . . losing his sight: previously prior of Westminster, he had been elected abbot of Bury in 1157 (*The Heads of Religious Houses, England and Wales 940–1216*, ed. D. Knowles, C. Brooke, and V. London, 1972, 32).

4 *William son of Isabel*: an important Christian moneylender and sheriff of London in 1176 and 1178–87; see H. G. Richardson, *The English Jewry under Angevin Kings* (1960), 59 and n. 2.

Isaac son of Rabbi Joce: of London. One of the key financiers of his day and the principal member of the London Jewish community. His father Rabbi Joce (or Joseph), who probably came from Rouen, had had extensive dealings with the Crown. Isaac was an extremely wealthy man, collecting the Crown's revenues in several shires; his possessions in Essex were confirmed to him by King Richard I in 1190. He died *c.*1200. See Cecil Roth, *A History of the Jews in England* (3rd edn. 1964), 7, 14, 31; and *Anglo-Jewish Letters 1158–1917*, ed. C. Roth (1938), 6–8.

Benedict the Jew of Norwich: the brothers Benedict and Jurnet (see below, p. 6 n.) of Norwich were major financiers of the Crown, operating from Norwich and London. Isaac son of Rabbi Joce worked in close co-operation with them. Roth, *History*, 10–11 n., 14–15.

letter from the king: Jews were in the special protection of the Crown, to which, when a Jew died, the debts owing to him were transferred. Hence the king's interest in Benedict's activities.

R. the king's almoner: possibly Roger, a member of the order of the Temple, appointed at Winchester *c.*June 1178 (*Recueil des Actes de Henri II*, ed. L. V. Delisle and E. Berger, 4 vols. 1909–27; Introduction, 451). The almoner supervised the distribution of the king's charitable gifts to religious institutions and to the poor.

5 *Archbishop Richard . . . our present exemption*: Archbishop Richard was made papal legate (the pope's representative in England) in April 1174, and as such carried out visitations of monasteries. As a result of Richard's visitation, Bury petitioned the pope for a clear exemption. This was granted to Abbot Hugh and the convent by Pope Alexander III on 23 Apr. 1175 (*Papsturkunden in England*, ed. W. Holtzmann, Abhandlungen der Akademie der Wissenschaften in Göttingen Philologisch-Historische Klasse, 3 folge no. 33, (1952), iii, no. 217). In future, only the pope himself, or a legate *a latere* (his personal representative, with full papal powers), might exercise such control over the monastery of St Edmund. See below, pp. 72–5 for Archbishop Hubert Walter's attempt to visit in 1195.

Master Geoffrey de Constantino: had been a prominent clerk in the households of Abbot Ording (1148–56) and Abbot Hugh (1157–80). A 'Master' was a person who had a university training.

H. and R. of Ingham: presumably the brothers Hugh and Roger of Ingham, who occur on pp. 45, 92, 108–9.

Acre: this seems more likely to have been the Cluniac priory of Castle Acre (about 35 miles from Bury), than the Augustinian house of West Acre (about 2 miles from Castle Acre), but the reason why Castle Acre was chosen as a place of exile is obscure.

6 *the cross . . . the 'Mariola' and the 'John'*: in his account of the fire of 1198 Jocelin records that these objects had been recently removed and so escaped the fire (see p. 95). It seems certain that they are identical; but either Jocelin is wrong in stating that they were a gift of Archbishop Stigand (d. 1072) or the author of the fourteenth-century 'Acts of the Bury Sacrists' is incorrect when he says that they were carved

('insculpi') by Master Hugo (who had made the great bronze doors at Bury) in 1130–40: perhaps they were further adorned or embellished in some way by Master Hugo. M. R. James, 'On the Abbey Church of S. Edmund at Bury', *Cambridge Antiquarian Soc. Publications*, Octavo ser. no. 28 (1895), offers no solution on this point (130, 133–4).

6 *Jurnet the Jew*: brother of Benedict of Norwich, who had lent money to the sacrist of Bury (above, p. 4 n.). Queen Eleanor of Aquitaine was also in his debt. On Jurnet and the Norwich jewry, see V. D. Lipman, *The Jews of Medieval Norwich* (1967), chap. 6.

Master Denis: probably the man mentioned above, p. 5 as having been exiled for a time by Abbot Hugh.

7 *pittancer*: the pittancer was the monastic official who distributed 'pittances' (small dishes of food, usually fish, eggs, or delicacies of some kind) in addition to the normal diet, on special days or for particular reasons, e.g. at bloodlettings (see below p. 14 n.) and to the sick: D. Knowles, *The Monastic Order in England* (1963), 463–4. For the Jews' refuge in the pittancery at Bury, see below, p. 10, and for Abbot Samson's suggestion that the monks should forgo their pittances to pay for repairs to St Edmund's shrine see below, p. 97

8 *Ranulph de Glanville, justiciar of England*: the justiciar's office was the greatest in the land. He presided over the Exchequer (the royal financial office) and the royal court in the king's absence, and acted as regent or viceroy when the king was overseas. Glanville himself had been active in Henry II's service as sheriff and judge, and was probably a considerable lawyer, although the treatise which has long gone under his name may not have been written by him (*The Treatise on the Laws and Customs of the realm of England commonly called Glanville*, ed. G. D. G. Hall (1965), xxx–xxxiii). He was appointed justiciar in 1179 or 1180, and continued in office until dismissed by Richard I in September 1189 (see F. J. West, *The Justiciarship in England 1066–1232* (1966), 54–63; cf. below, pp. 25, 46, 56, 65).

crossed the Channel to inform the king: the king was overseas in his Angevin dominions, and spent Christmas 1180 at Le

Mans; see R. W. Eyton, *Court, Household, and Itinerary of King Henry II* (1878), 237.

9 *Robert of Cockfield and the steward Robert de Flamville*: Robert of Cockfield, the descendant of an Englishman, held two knights' fees, several leased estates, and the half hundred of Cosford from the abbey. After his death in 1190, his son Adam was to claim the half hundred of Cosford as his by inheritance (pp. 52–3), and after Adam's death in *c.*1198, there was a further dispute over hereditary right in three manors, including Cockfield itself (below, pp. 109–10, 122–3). For the fees, see *English Historical Documents*, ii, ed. D. C. Douglas and G. W. Greenaway (2nd edn., 1981), 976, and below p. 107. The dispute over Cockfield is discussed by J. C. Holt, in *Transactions Royal Hist. Soc.* 5th ser. xxxiii (1983), 193–8.

As steward, Robert de Flamville acted on the abbot's behalf in the Liberty, especially in the administration of the courts. In 1182 the steward's office was claimed as hereditary by the Hastings family. See below, p. 25, and *The Kalendar of Abbot Samson*, ed. R. H. C. Davis (Camden 3rd ser. 84, 1954), l–li.

took securities: translated literally, this would read 'put under gage and pledge'. To gage was to provide security of property (hence 'mortgage') or money. To pledge was to provide another person to stand surety.

10 *narrative paintings and elegiac verses*: these paintings and their accompanying inscriptions may be those described in MS 30 of the Arundel collection in the College of Arms, London. They incorporated ninety subjects from the Book of Genesis, and encircled the choir-screen on the outside (James, *Camb. Antiq. Soc.* no. 28, 130–2), while painted hangings hung within. The screen was constructed to protect the monks from the cold during services.

11 *seven penitential Psalms*: Psalms 6, 32, 38, 51, 102, 130, 143.

Abbot Ording: previously monk, cellarer, and prior of Bury. He was Abbot Hugh's predecessor, elected abbot in 1138 but expelled on the return of Abbot Anselm in the same year. On Anselm's death in 1148 he was restored to the abbacy; he died in 1156 (*Heads of Relig. Houses*, ed. Knowles, 32).

12 *we ask Thee to hear us*: clearly here and elsewhere there are echoes of the Litany. *Norfolk trickster* may be a snide reference to Samson, who was a Norfolk man and about whom the expression is used below, p. 39.

14 *at blood-letting time*: the practice of blood-letting (using leeches) was common in monastic houses and was probably beneficial to the monks' health. It took place four or five times a year by *c*.1215 (Knowles, *Monastic Order*, 455-6). After blood-letting the monks did not immediately resume their normal routine. At St Albans, at about this date, two periods of conversation were expressly allowed in the parlour.

15 *Augustine . . . 10s. a day from the abbot's income*: Augustine (Eystein), a staunch supporter of Pope Alexander III, founded the cathedral of St Olaf at Trondheim (Norway). He fled to England in 1180 when Sverre Sirgurdsson captured Trondheim in his campaign against King Magnus: *Cambridge Medieval History*, vi. 300-1. He stayed at Bury from 9 Aug. 1181 to 16 Feb. 1182. The Pipe Rolls show that he was paid £94. 10s. over a period of twenty-seven weeks, confirming Jocelin's '10s. a day'.

the saintly boy Robert . . . recorded elsewhere: the death of the boy Robert, supposedly at the hands of the Jews, took place in 1181. Jocelin wrote his life, now lost. Similar deaths of children, which were alleged to have been ritual sacrifices by the Jews, took place in other cities, and cults grew up around them, as with St William of Norwich and 'little' St Hugh of Lincoln (see Roth, *History*, 13, 24-5).

16 *one side of the choir . . . the other*: the two sides of the choir, south and north, were controlled respectively by the abbot and the prior. Much of the liturgy was sung antiphonally, i.e. alternate verses by either side.

Four confessors: monks who had been ordained to the priesthood and so could act as confessors to the convent.

18 *William de Hastings*: presumably from the family that claimed the hereditary stewardship of the abbey (see p. 25).

19 *pleas of the crown . . . hundred courts*: for these disputes, see pp. 45-7 (pleas of the crown), 58-60 (scutages), 68-70

(market-place). The dispute over the hundred courts is not included in the Chronicle as it now survives. Sokemen were free tenants of middling status.

church towers . . . hundred years earlier: presumably a reference to the building works of Abbot Baldwin (1065–97). Abbot Samson saw to the completion of the great central tower of the western narthex, but it is not clear that there were western towers in Baldwin's church. A. B. Whittingham, *Bury St Edmunds Abbey* (HMSO, 1971), 6. See above, pp. 9–11 for Samson's activities as subsacrist, and above, pp. 63–4 for the bishop of Ely's thwarted attempt to obtain from Samson timber which was needed for the abbey's great tower.

Waltham: Bishops Waltham, where the bishop of Winchester had a residence, is about 10 miles south-east of Winchester.

Richard, bishop . . . and Geoffrey . . . York: Richard of Ilchester, an immensely influential royal servant of Henry II, was promoted to the see of Winchester in 1173. Geoffrey Plantagenet, the king's illegitimate son, was elected to the see of Lincoln in 1173, but declined to be ordained, being appointed royal chancellor. He was elected to the archbishopric of York in 1189.

20 *Master Nicholas . . . Bertrand . . . H[erbert] . . . monk of Bec*: all three men were Benedictines. Nicholas, who had been a monk of Malmesbury, was prior of Wallingford (Berks.), which was a dependency of St Albans. The priories of Horsham (Norf.) and St Neots (Hunts.) were alien houses, dependent respectively on the abbeys of Conches and Bec in Normandy. In 1183, the year after the Bury election, Nicholas became abbot of Malmesbury (Wilts.) and at about this time Bertrand became abbot of Chertsey (Surrey). Herbert remained prior of St Neots, last occurring there after 1189. *Heads of Relig. Houses*, ed. Knowles, 38–9, 97, 108.

22 *hastened to the altar*: the election had taken place in the king's chapel according to the terms laid down in the constitutions of Clarendon of 1164. See W. L. Warren, *Henry II* (1973), 477, and, for the text of the Constitutions, *English Hist. Docs.* ii. 718–22.

22 *blessed by the bishop of Winchester*: blessing by a bishop was an essential part of the ceremony surrounding the appointment of an abbot. Samson's blessing took place at Marwell, between Bishops Waltham and Winchester (*Memorials of St. Edmund's Abbey*, ed. T. Arnold (3 vols., 1890–6), ii. 5, where, however, the editor's note identifies Marwell incorrectly as on the Isle of Wight).

23 *a place where securities were given*: i.e. a law court.

Kentford: the abbey had land in Kentford, which lies at the extreme western edge of the Liberty on the road to Bury from Newmarket.

24 *more than a 1,000 dining together*: this impossible figure, as with many such figures in medieval literature, should be understood as an attempt to indicate a very large number of people.

a new seal . . . showing the mitre: several impressions of Abbot Samson's seal survive. See the facsimile in *Chronicon Jocelini de Brakelonda*, ed. J. Gage Rokewode (Camden soc. 1840), frontispiece, from a charter in the possession of the dean and chapter of Canterbury. This shows a standing figure in Mass vestments wearing a mitre, and holding a book in the left hand and a crosier, or crook, in the right. The counterseal (stamped on the reverse) is an *agnus Dei* (lamb of God). The use of the mitre on the seal signified a 'mitred' or highly privileged abbey, where the abbot took the place of the bishop.

25 *both lay and literate*: i.e. both laymen, such as barons, knights, merchants, the 'illiterate', and the 'literate' (*literati*), clerks or persons of some learning who knew Latin and might read and write. For the two stereotypes, see M. T. Clanchy, *From Memory to Written Record* (1979), 177–85. For the antagonism of the uneducated ('illiterate') monks towards the learned, see below, pp. 114–15.

came to do homage: as feudal lord of the barony of St Edmund, the new abbot summoned all those holding freehold tenancies to swear allegiance to him in the ceremony of homage, which created a bond of loyalty between lord and man.

not yet been knighted . . . steward: boys of knightly status were knighted, or 'dubbed', at the age of 15 or 16. For the duties of the steward, see above, p. 9 n.

26 *an aid*: in special circumstances, a feudal lord was entitled to request this tax from his tenants. The new abbot's first meeting with his knights was a suitable occasion for such a request.

twelve knights: this was the number of knights extra to the quota of 40 owed to the king (cf. pp. 58–60). Between 1166 and 1187, Henry II sought scutage from all 52 fees, although the abbot insisted that he owed on only 40; see H. M. Chew, *The English Ecclesiastical Tenants-in-Chief and Knight Service* (1932), 18–23, and *English Hist. Docs.* ii. 975–7.

birds of prey: Jocelin's word is 'kites', but it seems more likely that he means kestrels.

27 *letes, suits, hidages, foddercorn*: these were public obligations normally due to the king. In the Liberty of Bury they were due to the abbot as the king's representative. For purposes of taxation, the hundreds were divided into groups of villages, called 'letes'. 2s. was paid on the hide, and as each hundred was reckoned to contain 100 hides, 200s. was apportioned among the letes, each lete paying 13s. 6d., and the collector making a profit of 8s. 'Suit' was the duty of attending the hundred court. In the Bury hundreds, 'hidage' was a payment to the abbot, additional to rent. 'Foddercorn' was the provision of oats for the abbot's horses when he came to the hundreds (see *Kalendar*, pp. xv–xlvii).

short list . . . his 'Kalendar': the short list of knights was probably a copy of the return submitted to the king in 1166 (*English Hist. Docs.* ii. 975–7; for a list of 1200, see below, pp. 106–8). Although Jocelin implies that the Kalendar of revenues due to the abbot from the Liberty was written by 1186, the surviving text was composed between c.1186 and 1191 (see R. H. C. Davis's comments on the MS and on the date and purpose of the Kalendar, *Kalendar*, pp. ix–xv).

28 *silk copes . . . volumes bound in gold*: the cope is an ecclesiastical over-garment, like a semicircular cloak; and the dalmatic

a tunic traditionally worn by deacons. The thurible, or censer, is a metal vessel in which incense is burned: suspended by chains and with holes in the top, it is swung to release richly fragrant incense to 'cense' altars, church, and people, as a symbol of prayer. Precious gospel-books might be bound in gold and set with jewels: see Peter Lasko, *Ars Sacra: 800–1200* (1972) plate 222 for an example of 1170.

29 *recognition*: a payment made to a lord in acknowledgement of his lordship, usually at the beginning of a term of tenancy.

30 *carucate*: a measurement of land equivalent to a hide, which was traditionally the amount that could be ploughed by one ox-team in a day: perhaps about 120 acres.

31 *a judge delegate to hear certain cases*: Samson was to become a notable judge delegate during his career, being appointed many times by successive popes to hear specific cases in England. For the judge-delegate system, see J. E. Sayers, *Papal Judges Delegate in the Province of Canterbury 1198–1254* (1971).

liberal arts: the seven liberal arts—grammar, logic, rhetoric, geometry, arithmetic, astronomy, and music—were the basis of medieval education: the first three formed the *trivium* and the last four the *quadrivium*. The study of these subjects was preliminary to the study of Scripture. They were frequently depicted in art—in stained glass, manuscript illumination, and sculpture, as in the portals of Chartres and Laon cathedrals. See D. Knowles, *The Evolution of Medieval Thought* (1962), 73; and E. Mâle, *The Gothic Image*, trans. Dora Nussey (1961), 75–94.

a cultured man who had been at university: he had been at the schools (university) of Paris (below, p. 40), then the foremost centre of learning in northern Europe. Growing out of the cathedral school under William of Champeaux, it outstripped rival French cathedral schools by the mid twelfth century. It was William's pupil and bitter opponent, Peter Abelard, who established Paris firmly on the scholastic map. The majority of university-trained clergy in England in the second half of the twelfth century were probably graduates of Paris. See Hastings Rashdall, *The Universities of Europe in the Middle*

Ages, ed. F. M. Powicke and A. B. Emden (1936; reissued 1987), i. 275–8.

the Decretum and . . . decretal letters: the *Decretum* was the first major compendium of the church's law, being put together at the great medieval legal centre of Bologna in the early twelfth century. Copies of it were to be found in England by the middle of the century, and three Bury copies are known (see R. M. Thomson, 'The library of Bury St Edmunds in the eleventh and twelfth centuries', *Speculum*, 47 (1972), 641). *Decretal letters* were letters from the pope that answered particular legal points: they were collected together to form manuals for use by judges and others (see Sayers, *Papal Judges Delegate*, 34–7, and chaps. I and III).

itinerant justice: a travelling judge, who heard cases on behalf of the king at places outside London. See R. C. van Caenegem, *The Birth of the English Common Law* (1973), 19–22.

33 *the academic notion*: the text says 'the notion of the men of Melun'. In 1103 Peter Abelard had gone to Melun and established himself as a master there. The allusion may be to unorthodox teaching.

last night after Matins: the service of Matins began very early, and afterwards the monks returned to bed. The sequence of services was Nocturns (the night office), Matins (or Lauds), Prime, Terce, Sext, Nones, Vespers, Compline. For more details of the times of services, see Knowles, *Monastic Order*, 714–15.

master of the aumbry and librarian: an aumbry is a cupboard, in this case a book-cupboard, in which were stored books for immediate use in the cloister. Books were also found in other parts of the monastery. See *The English Library before 1700*, ed. F. Wormald and C. E. Wright (1958), chap. 2 'The monastic library'; and for the Bury library, see James, *Camb. Antiq. Soc.* no. 28, and Thomson, *Speculum*, 47, 617–45.

35 *hanapers*: hanapers were movable containers, often of wicker, from which the word 'hamper' derives. They were used especially for money, jewels, and other valuables, such as important sealed documents.

35 *entertainment of guests*: the remainder of this paragraph reads as if it is a verbatim copy of a document recording the abbey customs relating to hospitality. This was a topic on which there was a good deal of argument within the monastery; cf. pp. 6–7, and *The Customary of the Benedictine Abbey of Bury St Edmunds*, ed. A. Gransden (Henry Bradshaw Soc. 99, 1973), 5–7 and nn.

36 *the fall of Jerusalem*: the Crusaders' rule in the Holy City of Jerusalem, where they guarded the relics and sites of Christ's Passion, lasted from the time of the First Crusade, 1099, until 1187, when the city was recaptured by the Muslims, led by the 'Infidel' Saladin. This catastrophe caused widespread alarm throughout Christendom and led to the launching of the Third Crusade, of which King Richard I was a notable member. Jerusalem, however, was not to be recovered by the Christian armies. See H. E. Mayer, *The Crusades*, trans. J. Gillingham (1972).

37 *He could read . . . born and brought up*: see M. T. Clanchy, *England and its Rulers 1066–1272* (1983), 174–5, on the significance of this passage.

38 *on the king's behalf*: this repeats the story told on p. 8.

40 *Abbot Hugh's butler*: the butler in a feudal household was concerned with the provision of wine, and his office was usually hereditary.

40–1 *offences that carried fines*: these included non-appearance at court and non-payment of rent, and it is probably this kind of offence that is referred to here.

42 *excommunicated in every church and at every altar*: excommunication deprived the person against whom the sentence was pronounced of the right to receive the sacraments (or administer, if a priest). 'Greater' excommunication might also exclude him from all social contact with his fellow Christians. Sentences were widely publicized. See *Oxford Dictionary of the Christian Church*, ed. F. L. Cross and E. A. Livingstone (2nd edn. with corrections, 1983), 490.

the Great Roll of Winchester: a reference to Domesday Book, compiled in two volumes in 1086, which was kept in the royal treasury at Winchester, and which Jocelin mistakenly believed to be in the form of a roll, as indeed most Exchequer records were. For an account of the make-up of the two volumes of Domesday Book, see Helen Forde, *Domesday Preserved* (HMSO, 1986). For the Suffolk entries, see *Domesday Book*, vol. 34 (2 pts), *Suffolk*, ed. Alex Rumble (1986).

Queen Eleanor . . . 100 marks: 'Queen's gold' is first mentioned under Henry II as paid to his wife, Queen Eleanor. It was normally assumed to be a tax of 10 per cent on land transactions made with the king. Queen's gold appears to have formed an important part of the revenue of Queen Eleanor of Provence, wife of Eleanor's grandson, Henry III, in the mid-thirteenth century. See M. Howell, *Eng. Hist. Rev.* 102 (1987), 373–4.

King Richard's ransom: in 1193 the Emperor Henry V demanded a ransom of 150,000 marks of silver (£9,412. 10s.) for the release of Richard, who, on his way back from the Third Crusade, had been captured by Duke Leopold of Austria in 1192 and handed over to the emperor. A tax of 20s. on every knight's fee was taken, as well as a general tax of a fourth on revenues and movable goods. Religious houses were not exempt. Their plate was requisitioned; but some houses compounded in order to keep their valuables. By the end of 1193 enough money was raised to secure Richard's release, which took place on 4 Feb. 1194, although the full amount was never paid (A. L. Poole, *From Domesday Book to Magna Carta* (2nd edn. 1955), 362–6).

43 *new hospital at Babwell*: St Saviour's was founded by Abbot Samson in *c*.1184. It was just outside the north gate of the town. Two grants to it by Abbot Samson, including a grant of £20 from Icklingham, are printed in *Kalendar*, 88–90. On the Bury hospitals see *Victoria County History of Suffolk*, ii. 134–6. On hospitals in general there is still only Rotha M. Clay's *Medieval Hospitals of England* (1909).

dedication of our church: for the papal licence to dedicate, dated 1 December 1198, see *The Letters of Pope Innocent III (1198–1216) concerning England and Wales*, ed. C. R. and Mary G. Cheney (1967), no. 63.

43 *the election of Walter . . . bishopric of Lincoln*: Walter of
Coutances had been archdeacon of Oxford, and was keeper
of the king's seal, 1173–89. In the summer of 1184, a year
after his appointment to Lincoln, he became archbishop of
Rouen, and in 1191–3 acted as justiciar. Although called 'of
Coutances', he was born in Cornwall. See Poole, *Domesday
Book to Magna Carta*, 355–6.

the schism between Pope Alexander and Octavian: the anti-pope
Victor IV (Cardinal Octavian), the candidate of the emperor,
was elected the same day (7 Sept. 1159) as Alexander III, the
choice of the majority of the cardinals. He died on 20 Apr.
1164, and was succeeded by three more schismatic popes, all
candidates of the emperor. A general confirmation by Alexander III in favour of Bury and dated 12 Jan. 1162 at the
castle of Vada, on the Italian coast of Livorno, includes a
confirmation to the convent of Woolpit church 'when vacant'
(*Papsturkunden in England*, iii, no. 140). It is therefore likely
to be a confirmation of the bull acquired earlier by Samson.

44 *I pretended to be a Scotsman . . . a "gaveloc"*: although the
story suggests that the Scots recognized Octavian, all the
evidence is that Scottish envoys, who were in Rome at the
time of the election, plumped swiftly for Alexander. It is
possible, however, that the Scots did not remain staunch in
their support when they failed to get from Alexander exactly
what they wanted, namely metropolitan status for the bishopric of St Andrews. The English, on the other hand, delayed
recognition of Alexander until June/July 1160, but the king
is said to have given some people permission to go to Rome
late in 1159, and perhaps Samson was one of them; see M.
Cheney in *Eng. Hist. Rev.* 84 (1969), 474–92. '*Gaveloc*' is an
English word for a javelin or spear for throwing.

"Ride, ride Rome, turn Canterbury": this answer, deliberately
given by Samson in scarcely intelligible English, presumably
means 'I am riding to Rome and have nothing to do with
Canterbury'.

I held the letter beneath the cup: letters were often folded with
the *bulla*, or papal seal, protected inside, and when that was
done they might measure little more than 6 cm. square.

Geoffrey Ridel: a royal clerk who succeeded Thomas Becket as royal chancellor and archdeacon of Canterbury in 1162. Called by the Becket party 'the archdevil', he was made bishop of Ely in 1173. And see pp. 63–4.

although I had certainly not deserved punishment: the abbot was angry that Samson had arrived with the papal letter too late to prevent a royal clerk receiving the benefice.

45 *"spirituals"*: certain payments made to the bishop by the clergy.

45–6 *Archbishop Baldwin . . . liberties of our church*: murder was one of the 'pleas of the Crown' (i.e. serious offences reserved for judgment by royal justices), but in the Liberty of St Edmund, the abbot had the right to try such cases. The archbishop's refusal to acknowledge that the abbot had this right in the manor of Monks Eleigh, which (together with Hadleigh) was held by the monks of Canterbury, was regarded as a major threat to the integrity of the Liberty.

46 *The king . . . customarily possessed*: a charter to this effect, in which the king confirmed the rights of Bury within the Liberty against the monks of Canterbury, stating that he had not given to Canterbury any rights that belonged to Bury, is printed in *Feudal Documents of the Abbey of Bury St Edmunds*, ed. D. C. Douglas (1932), 105, where it is assigned to '*c*.1180'. It is so unusual in content, however, that there must be a very strong suspicion that it was concocted by the monks of Bury to use against the Canterbury claims.

47 *the bishop of Ely . . . at that time*: William de Longchamps, who was also papal legate, acted as King Richard's chief representative while the king was on Crusade, 1190–1. Although he was never actually given the title of justiciar, his power was so great that Jocelin obviously thought of him as such. Before Richard became king, Longchamps had served in his household in Aquitaine, and previously in Richard's brother Geoffrey's household. Apparently very ugly (he was likened to an ape and a hippopotamus), he received a bad press from the chroniclers for furthering his own aspirations and ruling tyrannically on behalf of Richard. There is no

doubt that he had designs on the see of Canterbury. See
Poole, *Domesday Book to Magna Carta*, 351–8.

47 *divine vengeance . . . forced to leave England*: the 'divine
vengeance', working through the opposition forces encouraged by the king's brother John, count of Mortain, forced
Longchamps to leave England in October 1191, after a period
of unrest and fighting in which he had faithfully defended
King Richard's cause.

48 *violence . . . at Dover*: the king's brother, Archbishop Geoffrey Plantagenet (in whose service Longchamps had once
been) was dragged from an altar in the priory of St Martin at
Dover, where he had taken refuge, and put in Dover castle
on the orders of the constable (Longchamps's brother-in-
law). Poole, *Domesday Book to Magna Carta*, 356.

canon of the Mass: the consecratory prayers, beginning 'Te
igitur', see *Oxford Dict. Christian Church*, 231–2; 'canon'
means fixed or unchanging.

taking the Cross: 'taking the Cross', vowing to go on crusade,
involved a ceremony of clothing in a garment on which a
cross had been sewn.

49 *identified him for certain*: adequate precautions needed to be
taken before the handing over of a large ransom, so that
identification, which often posed problems in an age before
the invention of photography, would have to be established
beyond doubt.

decrees against the black monks: this legatine council, presided
over by William de Longchamps at Westminster, 16 Oct. 1190,
is known only from chronicles. Both Jocelin and Richard of
Devizes record its attacks on the black monks. See *Councils and
Synods*, vol. I *A.D. 871–1204*, ed. D. Whitelock, M. Brett, and
C. N. L. Brooke (1981), pt. ii. 1029–31.

Count John . . . the siege of Windsor: in 1189 Richard I had
bestowed the comtè of Mortain (Normandy) on his younger
brother, the future King John (1199–1216), who during
Richard's captivity brought England into a state of war.
John's supporters occupied Windsor castle at the beginning
of the war (Poole, *Domesday Book to Magna Carta*, 364).

his own standard: reproduced in *Chron. Jocelini*, ed. Rokewode, 104, from Lydgate's fifteenth-century 'Life and
Miracles of St Edmund' (BL Harley MS 2278). It shows
Adam and Eve, with the serpent bound round a fruit-laden
apple tree surmounted by the *agnus Dei* against a starred
background. The Council of Westminster in 1175 had already
legislated against the bearing of weapons by religious (*Councils and Synods*, I. i. 988).

50 *tournaments to be held*: the writ of 22 Aug. 1194 allowed for
tournaments at five places: between Salisbury and Wilton
(Wilts.), between Warwick and Kenilworth (Warwicks.),
between Stamford and Warenford (Northumb.), between
Brackley (Northants) and Mixbury (Oxon.), and between
Blyth (Notts.) and Tickhill (Yorks.). The site between Thetford and Bury is not mentioned. Payments for this legalized
fighting were to be made to the king: earls were to pay
20 marks, barons 10, knights with land 4, knights without
land 2. On tournaments in general and the part they played
in cavalry training, see Juliet R. V. Barker, *The Tournament
in England 1100–1400* (1986), 17–27 (who does not, however,
correctly identify the Northumberland site), and on Richard's
personal interest in tournaments, see J. C. Holt, *Magna Carta
and Medieval Government* (1985), 81.

Archbishop Hubert [Walter]: archbishop of Canterbury
1193–1205; justiciar 1193–8; chancellor 1199–1205. He went
on Crusade with King Richard and was present at the siege
of Acre in 1191. And see below, pp. 72–5, 83, 101, 109.

50–1 *Immediately after his blessing . . . only for himself*: the three
privileges mentioned here are dated 31 Mar. 1183, 17 Jan.
1187, and 20 Jan. 1188 (*Papsturkunden in England*, iii, nos.
347, 399, 403).

51 *earl of Clare*: Ricard de Clare, earl of Hertford, lord of Clare
1173–1217 (*Complete Peerage*, rev. V. H. Gibbs, iii. 244, vi.
501–3).

Earl Aubrey [de Vere]: earl of Oxford, 1142–1194; king's
hereditary chamberlain, with lands in Suffolk and Essex
(*Complete Peerage*, x. 199–207). He held 5½ knights' fees of
the abbot (*English Hist. Docs.* ii. 976, and below, p. 106).

51 *Alfric . . . former lord of the hundred*: Alfric was the official who had administered the 8½ hundreds on behalf of Queen Emma, the mother of Edward the Confessor. See F. Barlow, *Edward the Confessor* (1970), 77 and n.

52 *Earl R[oger] Bigod*: earl of Norfolk, 1189–1221 (*Complete Peerage*, ix. 586–9). He held 3 knights' fees of the abbot (*English Hist. Docs*. ii. 976, and p. 106).

   Thomas de Mendham . . . belongs to him: he was one of Samson's senior advisers and he appears as one of the abbot's four constables shortly after 1200 (*Feudal Docs*., p. lxxxvi).

53 *Finally they came . . . his lifetime*: the agreement over the half hundred of Cosford, dated 29 Nov. 1191, is preserved in *Feet of Fines 1182–96* (Pipe Roll Soc. 17, 1894), 9–11, and an agreement over Groton and Semer is in *Kalendar*, 127–8. See also below, pp. 122–3.

   Herbert the dean . . . Haberdon: windmills and watermills were usually owned by feudal lords, who exacted a payment called 'mulcture' for their use. In Bury there were several mills belonging to the abbey, one of them very close to Haberdon, at the south gate (see above, Map p. vi, and M. D. Lobel, *The Borough of St. Edmund's* (1935), 20, 27), and it was these mills' exclusive rights that Samson was anxious to preserve. Herbert was a relative of Abbot Ording. He had two sons, Master Stephen (mentioned by Jocelin) and Adam. He provides an example of a married clerk in a period when church reformers had long been working to stamp out clerical marriage and impose celibacy. As dean, he was deputy to the abbey sacrist in his duties as monastic archdeacon, the abbey's disciplinary officer in church cases.

54 *moiety . . . portions . . . free alms*: the ownership of churches could be divided: a patron would make the presentation (or appointment) every second turn if he owned a half (moiety), and three times in every four if he had three-quarters. Land in free alms was held in return for the performance of spiritual services (i.e. prayers and masses), and in theory secular services, such as rents, were not supposed to be exacted from such land, although in practice they sometimes were.

an inquest . . . to decide about it: the assize of *darrein present-ment* provided that, if a dispute arose about the right of presenting a clerk to a church, an inquest of neighbours should be summoned to say who had presented last, and that person was adjudged to have the right to present. The aim was to find a quick solution. For a long-term settlement, a more detailed judicial process was required, initiated by a writ of right. F. M. Pollock and F. W. Maitland, *The History of English Law*, 2nd edn. revd. S. F. C. Milsom (1968), i. 148–9.

Durand de Hostesli . . . father-in-law: through his wife, Gun-nora, only daughter and heir of Robert of Valognes, Durand 'de Osteill' came into possession of the Valognes estates on his father-in-law's death in 1184. See I. J. Sanders, *English Baronies* (corrected edn. 1963), 12.

55 *Master Jordan de Ros*: he was parson of Harlow (Essex), and possibly a pluralist, as in 1175 he was the subject of a letter from the pope to Abbot Hugh allowing the abbot to give him a benefice (*Papsturkunden in England*, iii, no. 216). He was an Oxford Master; see A. B. Emden, *Biographical Register of the University of Oxford*, iii. 1591.

Archdeacon Walkelin: he was the bishop of Norwich's arch-deacon of Suffolk from before 1143 to January 1186. Hopton was on the northern border of the Liberty—hence Abbot Samson's jittery reaction. He did not want interference from the bishop of Norwich or his archdeacon.

Thetford priory: a Cluniac house in Norfolk, founded in 1103–4, which was about 10 miles from Hopton.

56 *an inquest in the royal court*: in this process, a jury was summoned to determine whether (*utrum*) the land was held by lay or spiritual tenure, i.e. lay fee or free alms. If the latter, the Church claimed jurisdiction over anything con-cerning it. Pollock and Maitland, *History of English Law*, i. 144–5.

56 *final agreement was as follows*: the remainder of the paragraph is based on a charter printed in *Kalendar*, 163–4.

56 *average price for grain*: as a large proportion of tithes consisted of grain, its price was of crucial importance in assessing the income of churches.

to swear . . . it was carried out: see p. 18.

57 *churches in the abbot's manors and socages*: unless otherwise stated, the following churches were in Suffolk. Most were in villages where the abbey had property at the time of Domesday Book (1086). A socage was an area of jurisdiction, where a lord might have granted away or leased out his estates, but still retained his overlordship.

Mildenhall . . . Wetherden—what shall I say about these?: the story of the recovery of Mildenhall in 1190 is told on pp. 41–3. For Wetherden, see pp. 84–5.

58 *staffacres and foracres*: probably small pieces of land not incorporated in the open fields, but lying at the edges; staffacres were probably enclosed by fences (staff = stave) and foracres were on the forelands, or headlands, which could not be ploughed as they were the turning-areas for the ploughs.

Barons of the Exchequer: the royal Exchequer was a law court as well as an accounting office and the judges who sat there were known as the Barons.

59 *Bigod . . . guard duty at Norwich castle*: in 1166 it was recorded that Hugh Bigod (Roger's father) refused to perform guard duty at Norwich castle, although ordered to do it by the king. See *English Hist. Docs*. ii. 977, and *Feudal Docs*. 99.

a copy . . . with the abbot: the court's copies of the separate agreements made between Samson and eighteen of his knights are printed in *Feet of Fines 7 & 8 Ric. I* (Pipe Roll Soc. 22, 1896), 40–6, 50–3, 86–8, and ibid. *9 Ric. I* (Pipe Roll Soc. 23, 1898), 37–8. The first is dated December 1196 and the last October 1197. Each knight promised the full amount of scutage and acknowledged castle-guard duty at Norwich: in return Samson pardoned any arrears.

60 *constabularies*: a constabulary was a fighting unit of ten knights, see *Feudal Docs*. pp. lxxxvi–lxxxvii.

recorded above: see p. 26.

'*wait fee*': a payment in lieu of guard duty.

each fast day of the four terms: the four terms were the 'quarter days'—Michaelmas (29 Sept.), Christmas (25 Dec.), Lady Day (25 Mar.), and the Nativity of St John the Baptist (Midsummer, 24 June), and the fast day of each was the day immediately preceding.

61 *The story of Henry of Essex*: this chapter heading is the only one for which there is manuscript authority, and it may be Jocelin's own caption to the story.

Henry of Essex . . . in a duel: Henry had been one of King Stephen's four constables, and continued in office under Henry II. In addition to military duties and responsibility for the payment of troops in time of war, the royal constables were in charge of the king's stables and the hunt. Henry held extensive estates in Essex and Suffolk, with a castle (of which the motte and bailey still survive) at Haughley, just outside the Liberty on the east (Sanders, *English Baronies*, 120–1, 139). Duel, or 'trial by battle', was a method of settling certain cases in this period. The dramatic story of the duel made its mark: as late as the reign of Richard I, a charter refers to land 'held on the day Henry of Essex fell in the duel' (J. C. Holt and R. Mortimer, *Acta of Henry II and Richard I Handlist*, List and Index Soc. spec. ser. 21 (1986), no. 349).

62 *Robert de Montfort . . . treason against the king*: the challenge to Henry of Essex was doubtless connected with an hereditary claim by Robert de Montfort to his constableship, as it had belonged to an ancestor who had been exiled by Henry I in 1107. But the king did not grant the constableship to Montfort after the duel, and he took Essex's lands into his own hands (Sanders, *English Baronies*, 120–1).

64 '*Elmswell*' . . . '*Elmset*' . . . *Melford*: Long Melford is the next parish to Glemsford, but Elmswell is more than 15 miles away to the north-east.

the reeves of St Edmund's town: the town formed part of the convent's property, not the abbot's barony, and the reeves were the convent's officers appointed to collect their dues and supervise the town. They were therefore not subject to the abbot's direction, as the sharp-minded justiciar, Ranulph de Glanville, pointed out.

66 *dispute . . . 'Mothorn'*: the 'Mothorn' was a horn for summoning the moot, or town assembly. The Faversham moot horn is a fine surviving example: see *The Age of Chivalry: Art in Plantagenet England 1200–1400*, ed. J. Alexander and P. Binski (1987), 280. At Bury it was not clear whether the prior, as head of the convent, or the sacrist, as lord of the borough, should present the 'Mothorn' and keys to the reeves (Lobel, *Borough*, 61–2). On this occasion the prior did so.

67 *canon law . . . abbot's control*: the ruling is in the *Decretum*; *Corpus Iuris Canonici*, ed. E. Friedberg (1879) i. 831, C. 18 q. 2 c. 9.

charter . . . from Henry II: this privilege was granted by Henry II, probably in 1155, but it seems to have been a confirmation of an earlier grant by his grandfather Henry I (1100–35). The sheriff of London had the power to take reprisals if the London merchants were charged tolls. See C. N. L. Brooke and G. Keir, *London 800–1216. The Shaping of a City* (1975), 40 and plate 10. Bury merchants themselves had these rights in markets and fairs, granted by Henry I in 1102, or 1103, 'through all my lands' (*Feudal Docs.* 62).

toll and team and all regalian rights: 'toll' gave the right to take toll on sales of any goods; 'team' gave jurisdictional rights over cases concerning stolen goods; 'all regalian rights' refers to the abbot's viceregal authority in West Suffolk.

68 *distraint*: distraint was a method of compelling someone to meet an obligation by seizing and detaining some item of their goods.

a former metropolis: although London had never been the seat of an archbishopric, the widely accepted but legendary history of Britain composed in the 1130s by Geoffrey of Monmouth made out that London had had metropolitan status in ancient times. See *Geoffrey of Monmouth: The History of the Kings of Britain*, trans. Lewis Thorpe (1966), 125, 172, 262.

69 *the charter . . . as he had promised them*: the surviving text, printed in *Kalendar*, 75–6, was issued some time between 1196 and 1200.

70 *tithing-pence*: it was customary to take a tax at the view of frankpledge, when the townsmen were summoned to the abbey's court to ensure that they were in 'tithings' (groups of ten men sworn to keep the peace).

Master Ranulph: he witnessed some of Samson's charters, was a tenant in Brettenham, and as parson of Westley was called by Samson 'our faithful clerk' (*Kalendar*, 58, 107–9, 113, 124).

72 *Abbot Robert of happy memory*: no details of the division are known, but the arrangement was confirmed by Henry I some time between 1108 and 1114 (*Feudal Docs.* 69). Such arrangements became the norm in monasteries in the twelfth century, to come into effect in a vacancy, during which, as at Bury, the convent—as well as the abbacy—might suffer exactions from the king's bailiffs if the properties were undivided. Knowles, *Monastic Order*, 614–15. See below, p. 80 for Abbot Robert's popularity at this time on account of this action.

74 *church of York*: Archbishop Hubert Walter had been granted legatine powers by Pope Celestine III on 18 Mar. 1195, not only over his own province, but also over that of York, which had been claiming exemption. In 1195 Hubert was acting as an itinerant justice in East Anglia, and so presumably tried to execute his legatine powers at the same time.

the pope added . . . exempt church: in a letter, dated at the Lateran Palace in Rome on 9 Jan. 1196 (*Papsturkunden in England*, iii, no. 477), Pope Celestine III reminded Archbishop Hubert that the abbey of Bury was subject to the pope alone and exempt from all legatine visitation except by a legate *a latere* (see above, p. 5 n.), and strictly forbade him to visit any exempt houses.

between Waltham and London: Hubert Walter was at Westminster on 18 and 19 Mar., and at Colchester on 23 Mar., *en route* for Norwich, *English Episcopal Acta*, iii, ed. C. R. Cheney and E. John (1986), 310.

76 *the French king*: Richard's long struggle to defend his Norman dominions against the ambitions of his overlord, Philip

Augustus, king of France, was renewed after Richard's release from captivity. See John Gillingham, *The Angevin Empire* (1984), 57.

76 *bishop of Lincoln*: the text reads 'the bishop of London', which must be an error for the bishop of *Lincoln*, Hugh, whose barony was seized in 1197 because of his refusal to send troops to Normandy (*The Life of St Hugh of Lincoln*, ed. D. L. Douie and D. H. Farmer, 1985, i, pp. xlii–xliv; ii. 98 ff.).

castle of Eu: a vital coastal fortress on the north-east border of Normandy, which had fallen to the French in 1193 but had been restored in the truce of 1196.

77 *buskins . . . crosier*: buskins were leg coverings made of silk. Those of Archbishop Hubert Walter survive: see *English Romanesque Art 1066–1200*, ed. G. Zarnecki (1984), 358 (with plate). The band of a crosier staff found in Samson's tomb is now in the Moyses Hall Museum, Bury. These items were part of the 'pontificals' or symbols of a mitred abbot. Samson had been granted use of the tunicle, dalmatic (a knee-length tunic), and sandals by Pope Urban III (*Papsturkunden in England*, iii, no. 385).

78 *debt of £50 by Michaelmas*: like the royal Exchequer, most medieval institutions used an accounting year that ran from Michaelmas, 29 Sept.

79 *Master G., a clerk of his own*: probably Master Gilbert of Walsham, who witnessed eleven charters between *c.*1196 and *c.*1211, printed in *Kalendar*.

80 *Abbot Robert's anniversary . . . Placebo and Dirige*: deceased abbots, monks, and benefactors were commemorated annually by the convent, usually on the anniversary of their death, with special masses, and also, not infrequently, with special dishes at table. The *Placebo* and *Dirige* (the origin of the word 'dirge') were parts of the Requiem service.

'*drunk*': the text gives '*bu*'; 'boozed' might be the best modern rendering of this French word. A Latin translation of this expression, as 'he went beyond the bounds of moderate drinking', was interpolated into Jocelin's text at this point.

81–2 *'I was his bishop . . . other poor people'*: 'I was his bishop' refers to Bury's privileged ecclestiastical jurisdiction over the town and *banleuca*, where the abbot acted as bishop. The clergy were responsible for overseeing the making of wills, whether written or verbal (nuncupative), as this one may have been, and for supervising the proper distribution of goods. If Hamo had not left enough to the poor to atone for his sins— and clearly 3 marks from 200 marks was a very paltry sum— the souls of both the dead man and his spiritual advisers were put in jeopardy. See in general M. M. Sheehan, *The Will in Medieval England* (1963), and especially on this case, 175 and 213.

82 *the canon sentenciae latae . . . by name*: At the Second Lateran Council in 1139, it had been declared that the sentence of excommunication took effect immediately the crime was committed, without trial and conviction before a court (*Corpus Iuris Canonici*, i. 822, C. 17 q. 4 c. 29), but the canonist Gratian and others did not accept this, holding that only named persons (i.e. those convicted by judicial procedure) could be anathematized. Samson, conversant with the law, clearly wished to leave no doubt about the excommunicate state of these men. See E. Vodola, *Excommunication in the Middle Ages* (1986), 28–32.

83 *reinstate the monks without further inquiry*: the monks had been ejected from the cathedral priory in 1190 by the bishop, Hugh of Nonant, who had replaced them with secular canons; see Knowles, *Monastic Order*, 322–4.

84 *using a book as a symbol*: in the transfer of land it was not unusual for an object such as a stick or clod of earth to be handed over, as a symbol for the land. A book constituted a similar symbol for the gift of a church.

Abbot Samson and Robert de Scales: the agreement survives in the *Feet of Fines 9 Ric. I*, 117–18; and a charter confirming it is in *Kalendar*, 145.

88 *confirmed in our charter*: printed in Lobel, *Borough*, 171–2, and for a discussion of these and the following events, see ibid. 29–30, 74, 81, 122–3.

89 *Abbot Ording . . . lies there*: abbots were commonly buried in the chapter-houses of monasteries.

lancetti of Hardwick: *lancetti* were tenants of lowly status, who held their land by a form of villein tenure, see Lobel, *Borough*, 20 and n., and cf. *Kalendar*, 52. Hardwick was a suburb of Bury.

90 *the penny called 'borthsilver'*: literally 'surety money', the same as tithing-penny (p. 70 and n.; cf. Lobel, *Borough*, 22, 35, and *Kalendar*, 136).

'averland': land held in return for the service of carrying the lord's goods from place to place, usually at set times of the year.

rood: a measurement of land that varied locally—perhaps about 30 square yards.

91 *'averpeni'*: a payment made in commutation of carrying services.

digging chalk or clay . . . fullers of the town . . . cloths he could find: 'fuller's earth', a kind of alum, was dug from the ground for use as a detergent in the process of fulling woollen cloth. The woven cloth was beaten and compressed in water, with fuller's earth, to shrink, thicken, and cleanse the fabric. See E. M. Carus-Wilson, *Medieval Merchant Venturers* (2nd edn., 1967), chap. IV, 'An industrial revolution of the 13th century'.

retting: the steeping of flax in water, to loosen the fibre from the woody core.

free bull: the right to own a bull, for whose service a fee would be taken, was one of the monopolies that belonged to the lord of the manor.

'hadgovel': or 'hawgable', a burgage rent of a penny on each house-plot in the borough. It was associated with ancient boroughs or towns of long standing. Lobel, *Borough*, 7–9, 54.

92 *scot and tallage*: town taxes.

⟨*Also, when herrings . . . . free of toll*⟩: this passage is misplaced here; it may be a later interpolation.

93 *escheats of lands . . . and widows*: when a tenancy came to an end for any reason, such as the dying out of a family, the land reverted to the lord as an 'escheat'. The heiresses and widows of deceased tenants were not able to marry without the lord's consent, for which a price was paid: their betrothal to ambitious men, prepared to pay highly, was a source of profit to the lord.

94 *pleas which belonged . . . of the suit*: cases which were to be heard by the abbot or convent had to be claimed in the county court; see R. C. Palmer, *The County Courts of Medieval England 1150–1350* (1982), 117–18.

the night of St Etheldreda: the liturgical day runs from Vespers to Vespers, so that the Feast of St Etheldreda, kept on 23 June, actually began on the evening of 22 June, and 'the night of St Etheldreda' was that of 22 June.

beat upon the board: a board was struck with a mallet as a signal to summon the convent: cf. *Customary of Bury St Edmunds*, ed. Gransden, 10 n. 4, 38 and n. 2.

the clock: in this period, clocks were driven by water.

95 *reliquaries . . . on the beam*: ornamented beams, on which stood reliquaries, were common in great churches. At Bury St Edmunds one such reliquary contained the hair and nail-clippings of St Edmund, which required cutting from time to time as his body was incorrupt.

99 *the discipline*: a scourge of knotted cords for the purpose of penance.

99 *albs*: white linen garments (symbolizing purity) which covered the whole body and were worn by ministers at Mass.

101 *salutations of the monk Ailwin*: Ailwin (Egelwin) had taken the holy body to London from 1010 to 1013, during the Viking raids, and served as its guardian. As an old man, some forty to fifty years later, when Abbot Leofstan opened the tomb, Ailwin was called upon to confirm the incorrupt state of the body (*Memorials*, i. 40–6).

night after the Feast of St Katherine: in modern terms, this is the night *of* the Feast.

103 *our serjeant Ralph the gatekeeper*: a serjeant was a tenant who performed some special service in return for his tenancy (or serjeanty). Ralph was a man of wealth and position; see *Kalendar*, 90 n. and index s.v. Ralph the porter.

corrody: board and lodging.

104 *'Ponder my words . . . as was customary*: chapter meetings closed with the chanting of Psalm 5, which was also part of the Office for the Dead.

106 *In the year . . . had been enfeoffed*: this survey was clearly an updated and amplified version of the list of knights' fees returned to the Exchequer by order of King Henry II in 1166 (*English Hist. Docs.* ii. 975–7; for a list drawn up a little after 1200, see *Feudal Docs.* pp. lxxxvi–lxxxvii).

parceners: the law of primogeniture applied only in the case of male children. If there was no son and more than one daughter, a landed inheritance was divided equally between the daughters, who were called 'parceners'. When married, their shares of the estate came into the possession of their husbands: presumably Arnold de Charneles was the husband of an heiress with sisters.

108 *Barton . . . rents*: the four manors belonged to the convent's portion of the abbey's estates (cf. above, p. 57).

109 *Archbishop Hubert . . . £100*: feudal lords often sold wardships of heirs and marriages of heiresses and widows in order to raise ready cash. Hubert Walter was quite a speculator in buying and selling wardships, making bargains for himself as well as his royal master in his capacity as justiciar and chancellor: C. R. Cheney, *Hubert Walter* (1967), 113.

Thomas de Burgh, brother of . . . the king's chamberlain: Thomas's brother Hubert began his career as chamberlain, in charge of the chamber, the king's private financial and secretarial office; later he became justiciar and earl of Kent. See *Complete Peerage*, vii. 133–42, where Thomas is mentioned, 133 n.

a charter . . . his lifetime only: presumably *Kalendar*, 127–8.

writ of recognition . . . before the king: the case to decide who was entitled to the land was heard at Tewkesbury in April 1201 (*Curia Regis Rolls*, i. 430). Cf. below, p. 122 n.

110 *abbot of Cluny . . . abbot of Chertsey*: Hugh V, abbot of Cluny (Burgundy) and head of the Cluniac Order, was in England at this time, 1201, perhaps because of the dispute over the patronage of Lewes priory (Sussex), a Cluniac house (*The Historical Works of Master Ralph de Diceto*, ed. W. Stubbs, Rolls ser. 68 (1876), ii. 173). Bertrand, abbot of Chertsey, had been one of the candidates for the abbacy of Bury in 1182 (see above, p. 20).

Robert the prior . . . close to death: he had been appointed in 1173, see above, p. 3.

116 *the dean of London . . . as follows*: Ralph de Diceto, from Diss (Norfolk), had been dean of St Paul's Cathedral since 1180, and was a prolific writer. Bury had a copy of his *Ymagines Historiarum*, and the version quoted by Jocelin is the author's unrevised text, which left St Paul's in 1198 (*Diceto*, i, p. xc). This passage is taken from Diceto's account of the events of 1175 (ibid. 401–2).

Another has said: we have not been able to trace the source of this quotation.

117 *monks of Ramsey . . . another house*: In both 1161 and 1180 Ramsey elected an outsider as abbot (*Heads of Relig. Houses*, ed. Knowles, 62).

abbot of Flay: Eustace, prior of Saint-Germer-de-Flay (Benedictine, dept. Oise, France), was a popular preacher who came to England in 1200 and again in 1201. He exhorted men to join a new crusade, inveighed against Sunday trading, and according to popular report performed certain 'water' miracles (for which see Cheney, *Hubert Walter*, 75–6).

117 *search . . . through his register*: a copy of the charter, dated 25 Mar. 1201, was entered in the king's charter rolls (*Rotuli Chartarum*, 1837, 91).

118 *Geoffrey Fitz Peter, the justiciar*: justiciar 1198–1213; earl of Essex 1199–1213 (*Complete Peerage*, v. 122–5).

119 *St Etheldreda's land*: St Etheldreda was the patron saint of Ely. A daughter of King Anna of the East Anglians, she was the first abbess of Ely, dying in 679.

119 *proposing to go abroad*: the abbot was among the ecclesiastics summoned by the king to Normandy in December 1201 (*Diceto*, ii. 173).

papal mandate . . . taken the Cross: once a person had taken the Cross, the oath had to be fulfilled unless absolution was obtained. The mandate is noted in *Letters of Innocent III*, ed. Cheney, no. 364.

122 *Appendix by William of Diss*: the following account, although not written by Jocelin, is appended to his chronicle in the MS. It may well have been prepared for use in the abbot's case in the Cockfield suit of April 1201 (above, pp. 109–10; and see Holt in *Trans. Royal Hist. Soc.* (1983), 194). William of Diss was chaplain (*Kalendar*, 146 *bis*, 148, cf. index s.v. William the chaplain), and was perhaps related to Master Walter and his father Master William (above, p. 40) and possibly also to Ralph de Diceto (of Diss; cf. above, p. 116 and n.)

123 *Lemmer*: Leofmaer, an Englishman (see *Feudal Docs.* pp. cxliii, 121).

	Classical Literary Criticism
	Greek Lyric Poetry
	Myths from Mesopotamia
APOLLODORUS	The Library of Greek Mythology
APOLLONIUS OF RHODES	Jason and the Golden Fleece
APULEIUS	The Golden Ass
ARISTOTLE	The Nicomachean Ethics
	Physics
	Politics
CAESAR	The Civil War
	The Gallic War
CATULLUS	The Poems of Catullus
CICERO	The Nature of the Gods
EURIPIDES	Medea, Hippolytus, Electra, and Helen
GALEN	Selected Works
HERODOTUS	The Histories
HESIOD	Theogony and Works and Days
HOMER	The Iliad
	The Odyssey
HORACE	The Complete Odes and Epodes
JUVENAL	The Satires
LIVY	The Rise of Rome
LUCAN	The Civil War
MARCUS AURELIUS	The Meditations
OVID	The Love Poems
	Metamorphoses
	Sorrows of an Exile

A SELECTION OF **OXFORD WORLD'S CLASSICS**

JANE AUSTEN	**Emma**
	Persuasion
	Pride and Prejudice
	Sense and Sensibility
ANNE BRONTË	**The Tenant of Wildfell Hall**
CHARLOTTE BRONTË	**Jane Eyre**
EMILY BRONTË	**Wuthering Heights**
WILKIE COLLINS	**The Woman in White**
JOSEPH CONRAD	**Heart of Darkness**
	Nostromo
CHARLES DARWIN	**The Origin of Species**
CHARLES DICKENS	**Bleak House**
	David Copperfield
	Great Expectations
	Hard Times
GEORGE ELIOT	**Middlemarch**
	The Mill on the Floss
ELIZABETH GASKELL	**Cranford**
THOMAS HARDY	**Jude the Obscure**
WALTER SCOTT	**Ivanhoe**
MARY SHELLEY	**Frankenstein**
ROBERT LOUIS STEVENSON	**Treasure Island**
BRAM STOKER	**Dracula**
WILLIAM MAKEPEACE THACKERAY	**Vanity Fair**
OSCAR WILDE	**The Picture of Dorian Gray**

The Oxford World's Classics Website

www.worldsclassics.co.uk

- Information about new titles
- Explore the full range of Oxford World's Classics
- Links to other literary sites and the main OUP webpage
- Imaginative competitions, with bookish prizes
- Peruse *Compass*, the Oxford World's Classics magazine
- Articles by editors
- Extracts from Introductions
- A forum for discussion and feedback on the series
- Special information for teachers and lecturers

www.worldsclassics.co.uk

American Literature

British and Irish Literature

Children's Literature

Classics and Ancient Literature

Colonial Literature

Eastern Literature

European Literature

History

Medieval Literature

Oxford English Drama

Poetry

Philosophy

Politics

Religion

The Oxford Shakespeare